SCIENCY-FUN WOWS!

54 SURPRISING BIBLE OBJECT LESSONS

for ages 3-7

Group

Loveland, Colorado
group.com

Group resources really work!

This Group resource incorporates our R.E.A.L. approach to ministry. It reinforces a growing friendship with Jesus, encourages long-term learning, and results in life transformation, because it's

Relational
Learner-to-learner interaction enhances learning and builds Christian friendships.

Experiential
What learners experience through discussion and action sticks with them up to 9 times longer than what they simply hear or read.

Applicable
The aim of Christian education is to equip learners to be both hearers and doers of God's Word.

Learner-based
Learners understand and retain more when the learning process takes into consideration how they learn best.

SCIENCY-FUN WOWS!
54 SURPRISING BIBLE OBJECT LESSONS
(for ages 3-7)

Copyright © 2018 Group Publishing, Inc. / 0000 0001 0362 4853

Visit our website: **group.com**

CREDITS
Contributing Authors: Kristen Kansiewicz, Lynn Lauterbach, Jessica Sausto
Chief Creative Officer: Joani Schultz
Editor: Jessica Sausto
Assistant Editor: Becky Helzer
Photographer: Rodney Stewart
Art Director: Jeff Storm
Lead Designer: RoseAnne Sather
Cover Designer: RoseAnne Sather
Interior Designer: Mollie Bickert

Scripture quotations are taken from the Holy Bible, New Living Translation, copyright © 1996, 2004, 2007, 2013, 2015 by Tyndale House Foundation. Used by permission of Tyndale House Publishers, Inc., Carol Stream, Illinois 60188. All rights reserved.

ISBN: 978-1-4707-5344-3

Printed in the United States of America.

10 9 8 7 6 5 4 3 2 1   27 26 25 24 23 22 21 20 19 18

INTRODUCTION

Science experiments are a surefire way to get kids' attention. Even better? When kids get to help! Supplement your Bible lessons with these Bible-related object lessons from the popular Dig In curriculum. Kids ages 3 to 7 will participate in exciting science fun that focuses on the life of Jesus, including these clever ideas:

- Using vinegar and baking soda to inflate a balloon (reminding them that Jesus heals the sick).

- Harnessing the power of static electricity to pick up various items (demonstrating Jesus' power over sickness and death).

- Testing homemade listening devices (a reminder that Jesus hears us).

- Putting a balloon on a fan and watching what happens (to learn that Jesus helps us believe in him, even though we can't see him).

These memorable object lessons will stick with kids for years to come! The Scripture and topical indexes make it easy to find an object lesson that goes with your Bible lesson.

Get ready for a lot of *oohs*, *aahs*, and *wows* as kids are amazed to see how science can illustrate important Bible truths.

Table of Contents

Continued ⟶

Table of Contents (continued)

AN ANGEL ANNOUNCES JESUS' BIRTH

Luke 1:26-38; Matthew 1:18-25

Supplies
- paper
- scissors

PAPER STRETCH

What Kids Will Do
Kids see a sheet of paper become taller than them.

Cut a Spiral
Hold up a sheet of paper for children to see.

Ask:

- **What things can you do with a sheet of paper?**

Say: **I'm going to do something really amazing—and kind of impossible. I'm going to make this sheet of paper taller than *any* of you.**

Ask:

- **Do you believe I can do that? Why?**

Cut a spiral shape—in a single, continuous cut—from the outer edge of the paper to the center of the paper. Make the cut about one-half inch wide. (The narrower the cut, the longer the spiral will be.)

As you cut, say: **God sent an angel to tell Mary and Joseph he'd send his Son,** Jesus, as a baby. To Mary and Joseph, that seemed *impossible*. But God does the impossible!

When you've finished cutting, ask a child to hold one end of the spiral to the ground while you hold the other end as high as you can.

Have children take turns jumping to see if the paper is taller than they can jump.

Talk About It
Ask:

- **What did you think when you saw me do something impossible with this paper?**

- **Why do you think God does impossible things?**

Say: **I had a plan for this little sheet of paper. I wanted it to do something big and amazing! God has plans, too... and sometimes he has to do something impossible to make those plans happen. God did something impossible when he sent his Son, Jesus. God does the impossible.**

God does the impossible.

THE FiRST CHRiSTMAS

Luke 2:1-7

Supplies

- large gift-wrapped box, with a removable lid that's also wrapped
- 6 paper lunch bags
- coins
- bell
- stuffed animal
- book
- strong-scented candle
- ball
- tape

Easy Prep

- Place each item in a separate paper lunch bag. Fold over the tops of the bags, and tape them closed. Place all the bags inside the wrapped box.

MYSTERY GIFTS

What Kids Will Do

Kids use their senses to guess mystery items.

Use Senses to Guess

Say: **The Bible tells us God sent his special Son as a gift to us. God sent Jesus to earth as a baby, and that's what we celebrate at Christmas because <u>Jesus is the best gift ever</u>. Let's think of other gifts we've received.**

It's fun to open gifts and look inside. When you get a gift, you probably like to look at it, feel it with your hands, listen to the noises it makes, and maybe even smell it! Let's use our eyes (point to eyes)**, our ears** (point to ears)**, our hands** (point to hands)**, and our noses** (point to nose) **to guess what's inside this gift box.** Pull the six bags out of the gift-wrapped box.

Hold up one bag. Say: **Let's guess what's in this bag by looking at it and feeling it.** Have the kids pass around the bag, looking at its shape and feeling it. Make sure they don't open it. As they pass around the bag, encourage them to talk about its shape, size, and feel—is it big

or small? Is it heavy or light? Is it round or square? Is it squishy or hard?

When the bag comes back to you, say: **Let's talk about what it sounds like.** Shake the bag, and have kids listen. Help them talk about what things make that sound.

Finally, open the bag and let kids sniff above the opening without looking inside it. Help them talk about whether they smelled anything.

Ask:

• **What do you think it is?** After several guesses, let a child pull out the item and show it to everyone. Have kids say whether they think it's a good gift.

Say: **Great job guessing what was in that bag! Now you know how to use your eyes** (point to eyes), **your ears** (point to ears), **your hands** (point to hands), **and your noses** (point to nose) **to guess. Let's guess what's in the other bags.** As time allows, lead the children to use their senses to guess what's in each bag. You can pass each bag to every child, or you can choose just a few children to explore the bag for

each sense. After children guess, reveal what's in the bag and have kids tell whether it's a good gift.

Talk About It
Ask:

• **What do you think makes a gift good?**

Say: **Good gifts might be things we like to play with; they might be soft and make us feel good; or they might be something we need. All of these things might be good gifts, but <u>Jesus is the best gift ever</u>. Jesus is a good friend, and he's fun and exciting to be around. He can help us feel better when we're sad. And he gives us everything we need. Like we looked at the bags, we can look for ways Jesus is the best gift, and we can listen for ways <u>Jesus is the best gift ever!</u>**

Jesus is the best gift ever.

JESUS, THE LIGHT OF THE WORLD, IS BORN

Luke 2:1-20

NEED THE LIGHT

What Kids Will Do
Kids show love in various ways with their eyes closed.

Try Without Light
Say: **Jesus is the light of the world, and he came to show us God's love. Let's have fun showing love to our friends.**

Have kids scatter around the room so they're as far apart as possible. Dim the lights, and ask children to cover or close their eyes tightly—and keep them closed!

Call out the following tasks one at a time, reminding children to keep their eyes closed or covered the whole time:
- hug a friend
- kindly pat someone on the back
- give a high-five
- find a friend and say "Jesus is the light of the world!"

Celebrate Jesus
Let children open their eyes, and have them form a circle on the floor.

Say: **It looked like you had some trouble showing love.**

Ask:
- **Why was showing love hard?**

Say: **When God sent Jesus to be born, it was like God saying, "I love you so much that I'm sending my very own Son to help you!" Jesus was like a light, shining God's love to people who felt sad and lonely. Jesus is the light of the world.**

Turn on the lights. Say: **Now that we have light, let's play our game again!**

Repeat the activity, but keep the lights on and let kids keep their eyes open. Each time kids show God's love to a friend, call out "Jesus is the light of the world!"

Say: **The light made a big difference! Jesus is the light of the world, and that makes a big difference in our lives every day.**

Jesus
is the light
of the
world.

SIMEON AND ANNA SEE JESUS

Luke 2:21-40

Supplies

- tape
- scissors
- small gift box
- black wrapping paper
- 2 different colors of shiny or metallic wrapping paper
- Starburst candies (1 per child)
- "Picture of Jesus" handout (1 copy) (p. 17) (available in color at ww2.group.com/reproducibles)

Easy Prep

- Fill a small gift box with Starburst candies, enough for each child to have 1. Tape the picture of Jesus inside the lid of the box.
- Wrap the gift box in 3 layers of wrapping paper. The first 2 layers should each be a different color of shiny or metallic paper, and the outer layer should be black wrapping paper. When you add the second and third layers of wrapping paper to the box, be sure to avoid taping to the previous layer so it will be easier for kids to pull off pieces of only 1 layer of wrapping paper at a time.

GIFT UNWRAPPED

What Kids Will Do

Kids unwrap a gift that has many layers of wrapping paper.

Unwrap the Box

Have kids sit in a circle. Say: **God sent Jesus to us as a very special gift. God loves us so much, and he wants to be with us all the time—in happy times and in sad times.**

Hold up the gift box wrapped in black paper.

Say: **This gift box doesn't look very cheerful or happy. It reminds me of some of the sad or dark times we go through. <u>Jesus is God's gift</u> who came to help us through sad, dark times. Let's work together to get rid of this black paper!**

Tear off a small piece of the black paper, revealing the shiny paper underneath. Pass the box around, and let each child tear off a piece of the black paper. Each time a child tears off some of the black

paper, lead kids in saying "Jesus is God's gift!"

When the box comes back to you, set it in front of you. Point out that the box is pretty, but it's still wrapped—so kids will still have to wait to open the gift.

Say: **Simeon and Anna waited a long, long time to see God's gift—Jesus. Let's take our time and slowly take the paper off to see what's underneath.**

Tear off a strip of wrapping paper to reveal yet another layer of wrapping paper. Pass the box around, and let each child tear off a piece. Each time a child tears off a piece, lead all the kids in saying "Jesus is God's gift." When the box comes back to you, set it in front of you. Point out that it looks as if kids will *still* have to wait!

Reveal the Surprise Inside
Ask:
- **How did you feel when you saw *another* layer of paper underneath?**

Say: **It's so hard to wait! I think Simeon and Anna were excited to see Jesus, and *this* gift looks bright and exciting! Let's peel off the last layer of paper. When it's all off, I'll open the box so we can see what's inside.**

Pass around the box, and let kids take turns tearing off pieces of paper. When the box comes back to you, open it and show children the picture of Jesus.

Say: **I'm so excited! *We* don't have to wait for the gift of Jesus. Jesus has already come, showing each of you God's wonderful, sweet, surprising love. Jesus is God's gift to *all* of us. Jesus wasn't just a special person—Jesus was God's very own Son! There's something else in here, too!**

Take out the Starburst candies. Give a candy to each child, and as you do, pray: **Thank you, God, for giving Jesus as a gift to** [child's name].

Jesus is God's gift.

PICTURE OF JESUS

WISE MEN WORSHIP KING JESUS

Matthew 2:1-18

Supplies
- birdseed
- glue
- crayons
- paper bowls
- "Newborn King" handout (1 copy per child) (p. 19)
- real or artificial plants

Easy Prep
- Fill several paper bowls with birdseed and place them on a table.
- Set a few real or artificial plants on the table.

GROWING A KING

What Kids Will Do
Kids explore how seeds grow into plants.

Feel Seeds and Plants
Have each child take a seed from one of the bowls. Encourage kids to examine the seeds in their hands.

Ask kids to take turns finishing this sentence: "This seed is…" Encourage kids to think of as many descriptions as possible, such as *small, tiny,* or *round.*

Have children put the seeds back in the bowl, and let them touch a plant.

Say: **Plants like this start out as teeny, tiny seeds. But the seeds change and plants grow from them. In the same way, people start out as tiny babies, and those babies change and grow.** *You* **started out as a baby. But you grew and are still growing. When the wise men found Jesus, he was very small and young—younger than you are! But the wise men knew <u>Jesus would grow up to be the King</u>.**

Talk About It
Give each child a copy of the "Newborn King" handout.

Let kids color the picture. Then help kids each place a dot of glue anywhere they'd like on the picture and put a seed on the glue. While children work, talk about what *they* might be when *they* grow up. Point out that God has big plans for them, and God will be with them as they grow.

Jesus is the King.

NEWBORN KING

JESUS SPEAKS WITH THE RELIGIOUS TEACHERS

Luke 2:41-52

Supplies
- various nonfiction picture books on different subjects such as animals, cars, or trains. (If you don't have these available at your church, you can find them at the local library.)

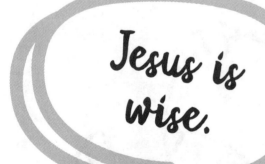

Jesus is wise.

JESUS KNOWS EVERYTHING

What Kids Will Do
Kids explore books on various nonfiction subjects.

Look for Books
Have kids sit in a circle around a pile of the books.

Say: <u>Jesus is wise.</u> **That means he always knows what to say and do. Jesus really knows a lot! When we read books we can know a lot, too.**

Hold up a book.

Ask:
- **What kinds of things can you learn from this book?**

Say: **If we read all these books, we would know a lot!**

Ask:
- **If we want to know about** [name one subject that's tied to one of the books], **which one of these books would we read?**

Choose two or three kids to look through the books to find the subject you mentioned.

Say: **This book can help us know about** [subject]. Explain how learning *about* that subject can help you be wise. For example, if the book is about horses, kids can learn how to know when a horse is hungry and what horses like to eat.

Continue asking children about different subjects, and let them find the books that match those subjects. Connect each subject to what you can do when you know a lot about that subject.

Look to Jesus
Point to the pile of books.

Say: **These books can help us know about** [say a few subjects that are tied to the books]. **But these books can't help us know about everything. If we read all these books, we still won't know** *everything.*

Do you know who does know everything? Jesus knows everything! Jesus is wise. When he was still a child, Jesus stayed in church when his family left so he could keep learning.

Share something *you* want to learn about, and then tell kids that Jesus knows all about that.

Ask:
- **What's something *you* want to learn about?** After each idea that a child mentions, say: **Jesus knows all about that!**

Share something *you* want to learn to do, and then tell kids that Jesus could do it if he wanted to.

Ask:
- **What's something *you* want to learn to do?** After each idea that a child mentions, say: **Jesus knows how to do that!**

Say: **Jesus knows everything. He always knows what to say and do. He knows all about you, and he knows all about me. He knows what makes you happy and what makes you sad. He knows what you need and he knows how to help you. And you can ask him to help you know what to do, because** <u>Jesus is wise.</u>

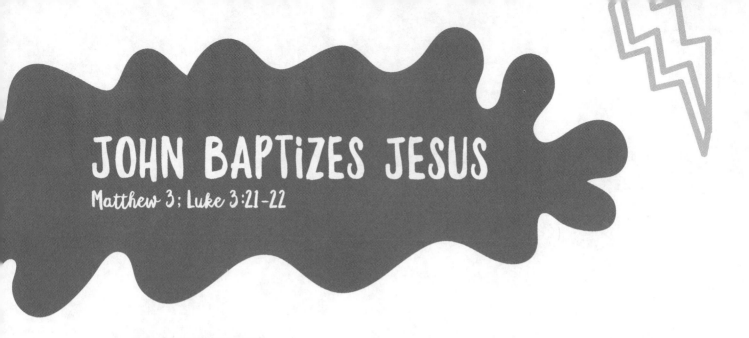

JOHN BAPTIZES JESUS
Matthew 3; Luke 3:21-22

Supplies
- large box
- 1 large building block and 1 small building block
- 1 large ball and 1 small ball
- 1 large book and 1 small book
- 1 large stuffed animal and 1 small stuffed animal
- 1 paper towel roll and 1 paper towel sheet
- 1 bottle of water and 1 empty clear cup

Easy Prep
- Put all the items in the box.

HOW ARE THEY ALIKE?

What Kids Will Do
Kids play with like items.

Compare Items
Say: <u>Jesus is God's Son.</u> **That means Jesus is like God.**

Tell about someone *you're* like. If possible, tell how you're like your father.

Ask:

- **Who is someone *you're* like?**

Show the box. Say: **I have some things in this box that are like each other, kind of like Jesus and God are like each other.**

Show the large and small building blocks, and have kids tell how they're alike.

After several things are mentioned, say: **Like these blocks, Jesus and God are like each other in many ways because <u>Jesus is God's Son</u>.**

Show kids each pair of items that are alike, having them discuss how they're alike. (For the water, you can pour a small amount from

Jesus is God's Son.

the bottle into the cup.) As you show each pair of items, remind kids that Jesus and God are alike because <u>Jesus is God's Son</u>.

Match Items

Put all the items back into the box.

Hold up the box, and invite one child to grab one item from the box without looking. Have the child show it to the other children in the group.

Invite a different child to find the item that's alike by looking through the box. After the child shows the match to the group, say: **Jesus and God are like each other, too.** Then have the children say "<u>Jesus is God's Son</u>!"

Let other children take turns as time allows.

Talk About It

Say: **When John the Baptist baptized Jesus, God came and told everyone listening that Jesus is his Son. If <u>Jesus is God's Son</u>, that makes Jesus and God very much like each other.**

Ask:

* **What makes a son like his dad?**

Say: **Jesus is like his dad, too. Jesus has his dad's power and strength, and Jesus is perfect like his dad—and that makes God happy.**

SATAN TEMPTS JESUS

Matthew 4:1-11; Mark 1:12-13; Luke 4:1-13

Supplies

- blue sticky notes
- sticky notes in at least 2 colors other than blue
- stickers
- undesirable items, such as an obviously dirty sock, a broken toy, and a plate with a few cookie crumbs (1 item for each pathway that's not blue)

Easy Prep

- Hide the stickers in 1 place in your room.
- Place blue sticky notes on the floor to make a path that leads children to the stickers. Make the path travel to different areas of the room before it takes kids to the stickers.
- Use a different color of sticky note to make a different path that leads to each of the undesirable items. (Although the items will be at the end of the paths, put them slightly out of sight so kids won't know what the items are until they get there.) Have these paths cross the blue sticky-note path a few times.

FIND YOUR WAY

What Kids Will Do

Kids follow different paths, looking for the right one.

Try a Path

Say: **There are stickers in this room—one for each of you! But we have to find the right way to get to them. Which color pathway do you want to follow?** Encourage kids to yell out their choices, and choose one child who didn't say "blue."

Let one child lead the others along the first color path. When you get to the end, point out that there are no stickers at the end of that pathway. Ask the children if they want the item that *is* there.

Invite the children to choose a different pathway, and lead children to choose one other than blue. Let a different child lead the others along that path, and point out that there are no stickers

Jesus shows us the right way.

when the children reach the end. Ask the children if they want the item that *is* there.

If you have other color pathways, let kids try those, and then try the blue pathway last. When you get to the end of the blue pathway, help the children find the stickers.

Say: **The blue pathway showed us the right way to the stickers. The blue pathway was like Jesus because <u>Jesus shows us the right way</u>. The other pathways took us in the wrong direction! They didn't get us to where we wanted to go. We want to take each step in the right direction, or the right way.**

Talk About It

Share why *you* want Jesus to show you the right way when you're making choices.

Ask:

- **Why do *you* want to make right or good choices?**

- **What do *you* like about getting Jesus' help to make right or good choices?**

Say: **<u>Jesus shows us the right way</u>. When God's enemy tried to get Jesus to make wrong choices, Jesus knew what was best. Jesus knows the way that's best for us, too! That's why we ask him to help us know the right way.**

25

JESUS CALLS DISCIPLES
Mark 1:16-20; John 1:35-51

Supplies
- yellow, blue, and red finger paints
- paper
- wet wipes
- smocks

COLOR CHANGES

What Kids Will Do
Kids mix colors and watch them change.

Mix Colors
Have children put on smocks, and give each child a sheet of paper.

Say: **When Jesus became friends with Simon, Andrew, James, John, and all his disciples, he changed their lives. He helped them follow him, and he made their lives better. <u>Jesus can change our lives</u>, too. He can make our every day new and better. Let me show you what I mean.**

Hold up the yellow paint. Say: **I can help you *change* this yellow paint to a *new* color! I'll change it so it's not yellow anymore. Do you believe me?** Let the children respond. If any children do think you can change the color, let them guess what color it will change to.

Put some yellow paint on each child's paper. Say: **Here's how we'll change it to a new color: We'll just add blue.** Add some blue on top of each child's bit of yellow, and have

Jesus can change our lives.

children mix the two colors with their pointer fingers until it changes to green.

Say: **It's not yellow anymore. And it's not blue anymore. Now it's green! Do you want to make some other colors change into new colors?**

Continue leading children to make new colors, letting them guess the color change before mixing. Red and yellow make orange. Red and blue make purple. Kids can also mix colors into the already-mixed colors to see how they'll change.

Talk About It

Tell what *you* like about colors changing.

Ask:

- **What did *you* like about the color changes?**

Say: **When we mixed the colors, they changed. We made new colors. Like that, when we spend time with Jesus, he changes us. He makes good and surprising changes in our lives. He makes us new. He makes our every day better!**

JESUS PERFORMS HIS FIRST MIRACLE

John 2:1-12

Supplies

- flashlight with batteries
- red cellophane (check the gift wrap section of hobby and discount stores)
- rubber band
- 8-ounce clear plastic water bottle with a lid (empty)
- funnel
- water

Easy Prep

- Place red cellophane over the end of a flashlight. Use the rubber band to hold it in place. Check that it shines with a red tint. If it doesn't, add more layers of red cellophane.
- Tape the bottom of the water bottle to the light end of the flashlight.
- Remove the batteries from the flashlight and keep them on hand but out of sight.

POWER SOURCE

What Kids Will Do

Kids see water change colors.

Try to Turn On the Flashlight

Say: **Jesus has God's power! He can do anything God can do. When someone's sick, Jesus can make the person healthy. When there's a storm, Jesus can make it stop. Let's do something to help us think more about Jesus' power.**

Tell about a couple of things that give power, such as electricity or gasoline.

Ask:

- **What are some things that have power?**

Hold up the flashlight, and then have a few kids try to turn it on.

Say: **A flashlight won't work without batteries. A flashlight gets power from the batteries. If we put batteries in a flashlight, we can turn on the light. The batteries give power just like God gives power. Jesus gets his power from God.**

Jesus has God's power.

Insert the Power

Show kids the batteries, and have them watch while you put them into the flashlight. Darken the room as much as possible, but don't turn on the flashlight yet.

Say: **Because <u>Jesus has God's power</u>, he changed water into a different drink. At a wedding, Jesus had servants fill big containers with water.**

Carefully hold the flashlight as you pour some water through the funnel into the water bottle. Put on the lid. Point out that the water didn't change like it did for Jesus.

Say: **Jesus isn't just an ordinary person like us. <u>Jesus has God's power</u>. Let's use the power in this flashlight to try to change the water.** Turn on the flashlight so the cellophane gives the water a red tint. Let each child turn the flashlight on

and off, and assist any kids who need your help.

Say: **Like the batteries give the flashlight power to make this water change colors, <u>God gives Jesus power</u> to do anything he wants or needs to do.**

Tell some things Jesus can do with God's power.

Ask:

• **What do you think Jesus can do with God's power?**

Share why *you* believe Jesus uses his power to take care of you.

• **What ways can Jesus use his power to take care of *you*?**

Say: **Jesus loves you, and you can trust him to use his power to take care of you!**

NICODEMUS VISITS JESUS AT NIGHT

John 3:1-21

Supplies

- 8x1-inch strips of paper (about 12 per child)
- stickers (several per child)
- tape

FOREVER CHAINS

What Kids Will Do

Kids make circles with strips of paper.

Make a Circle

Give each child one strip of paper. Have kids each decorate their strips with a sticker or two and then tape the ends together to make a circle.

Say: **A circle can remind us that <u>Jesus gives us eternal life</u>. A circle is a shape that can help us think of forever because we can't tell where a circle starts or ends.**

Have the children trace their fingers around their circles. Say: **Your circle can help you remember that <u>Jesus gives us eternal life</u> because Jesus makes it so that we can live forever in heaven with him!**

Make a Circle of Circles

Have kids each put a couple of stickers on several additional strips of paper (at least 10 strips per child). Then show them how to make a chain by sticking a strip through the circle before taping it shut. When kids have made a reasonably long chain, take one more strip of paper and stick it through the two end links of the chain, taping it shut and making a big circle.

Say: **Now you have one big circle made out of a lot of little circles! Can you find the beginning or end of the circle chain?**

Have kids look, but they'll be unable to find a beginning or end.

Talk About It
Ask:

- **What's your favorite shape?**

Tell a couple of things that make circles different from squares or triangles.

Say: **There are a lot of fun shapes, but we can look at circles as a reminder that if we believe in Jesus, we'll live forever with him! When Jesus talked to Nicodemus, he tried to help him understand eternal life. It's okay that it's a little confusing! But when you see a circle, just remember: <u>Jesus gives eternal life</u> with him. That means a life that never ends!**

Jesus gives us eternal life.

JESUS IS REJECTED

Luke 4:16–30

Supplies

- votive candles
  (1 for every 10 kids)
- small or medium glass plates
  (1 for every 10 kids)
- canning jars or clear glasses
  (1 for every 10 kids)
- lighter or matches
- water
- blue food coloring

Easy Prep

- Color about 2 tablespoons
  of water for every 10 kids.
  You'll need only 1 or 2 drops
  of food coloring for every 2
  tablespoons. You want the
  water to be visibly blue.

Jesus loves everyone.

GATHERED TO JESUS

What Kids Will Do

Kids watch something amazing happen with water.

Watch the Water Move

Say: **The Bible says <u>Jesus loves everyone</u>. One time Jesus was at a place like church, and he read the Bible to the people there. He shared how much he loves everyone and that he came to earth to be with us. Let's do something really neat to help us think about what that means.**

Have every 10 kids gather around a plate with an adult or teen helper.

Pour a couple of tablespoons of colored water onto the plate, and then place the candle in the center of the puddle. Say: **This candle is really powerful—it can do something pretty special with this water. Let's watch.**

Let the children get a look at the setup, and then have them sit about 2 feet away from the plate with their legs crossed and their hands in their laps. (Avoid being in the way of any child's view of the candle.)

When everyone has settled, light the candle and place the canning jar upside down over the lit candle. Have adult or teen helpers do the same for other groups. Within seconds, the heat from the flame will draw the water underneath the jar and the flame will be extinguished.

Say: **Wow! All the water moved into the jar!** Let the children view how the water is surrounding the candle inside the jar.

Repeat the process more than once if kids want to see it again. Simply remove the jar and the water will spread out into a puddle again.

Talk About It
Say: **The candle pulled the water into the jar so the water was all around the candle! Jesus is like the candle. He pulls us to him like the candle pulled the water to it. Jesus wants every one of us to be with him. That's because <u>Jesus loves every one</u> of us!**

TIP!

Be sure kids sit a couple of feet away from the plates to prevent them from being close to the candle. Do not let the children touch the candle, lighter, or matches.

JESUS HEALS PEOPLE

Luke 4:38-40; 5:12-16

Supplies

- distilled white vinegar
- baking soda
- empty water bottle
- uninflated balloon
- permanent marker
- funnel

Easy Prep

- Pour 1 to 2 inches of distilled white vinegar into the empty water bottle.
- Inflate the balloon, but don't tie it off. Use the marker to draw a fairly detailed face on the balloon, and then let the air out of the balloon.
- Use the funnel to fill the limp balloon halfway with baking soda, and then set it aside.

REVIVE THE BALLOON MAN

What Kids Will Do

Kids see a balloon inflate in an amazing way.

Revive the Balloon Man

Say: **Jesus helped many people. He healed a sick woman so she wasn't sick anymore. He healed a lot of sick and hurt people so they would get better. Jesus heals people today, too.**

Twist the end of the balloon so the baking soda doesn't leak out. Hold it upright, and show kids the face on the balloon.

Say: **This balloon man is sick, too. He has no air in him, and that makes him sad. Balloon men always like to have air to fill them and make them big and round. Let's see if we can help him get some air.**

Without letting any of the baking soda get into the bottle, carefully place the end of the balloon fully over the mouth of the water bottle.

Say: **When Jesus made the people better, it was a big surprise. No one could heal people** without Jesus' help. It was really special and amazing—kind of like this. Watch!

Hold the balloon upright so all the baking soda falls into the bottle at once. Be sure to keep the end of the balloon fully covering the opening of the water bottle by holding the balloon tightly at the mouth of the bottle. The reaction of the vinegar and the baking soda will cause the balloon to fill with air. When the balloon is inflated, remove it from the bottle, pinching the end and tying it off to keep it inflated.

Talk About It
Ask:

- **What did you think of how our balloon man filled with air?**

Say: **It was really neat to see how the balloon man filled with air. We made the balloon man happy because he didn't have any air in him and now he does. Jesus did some amazing things, too.**

Ask:

- **When Jesus made the sick people better, what did you think of how they felt?**

Sing and Play
Say: **Let's sing a song to celebrate how <u>Jesus heals us</u>, kind of like how we helped the balloon man.**

Have kids sit in a circle. Teach kids the following lyrics to the tune of "Do You Know the Muffin Man?" before singing the song while they bop the balloon around the circle. Play as time allows.

🎵 **Do you know that Jesus heals, That Jesus heals, that Jesus heals?**

Oh, do you know that Jesus heals Through the power of God?

Oh yes, I know that Jesus heals, That Jesus heals, that Jesus heals. Oh yes, I know that Jesus heals Through the power of God!

Say: **What we did to help our balloon man was pretty amazing. But what Jesus did to heal the people was way more amazing and very special. He made people better when they were sick. He fixed things that were broken. Jesus is amazing and powerful! And <u>Jesus can use his power to heal us</u>, too.**

Jesus heals us.

JESUS FORGIVES A PARALYZED MAN

Luke 5:17-26

Supplies
- sugar cubes (at least 4 per child)
- empty clear plastic water bottles with lids (1 per child)
- water at room temperature

Easy Prep
- Fill the water bottles about ¾ full, and replace the lids.

DISSOLVING SIN

What Kids Will Do
Kids watch sugar cubes dissolve.

Dissolve the Sugar Cubes
Say: **We can read in the Bible about how Jesus helped a man so he was able to walk. But Jesus also forgave him. Jesus knew the man had done wrong things, but Jesus forgave him. It was like Jesus made the wrong things he'd done disappear. I'll show you what I mean.**

Hold up a sugar cube. Say: **I can make this sugar cube disappear like Jesus made the wrong things the man did disappear. Watch me!**

Show kids the water in the water bottle, and then drop the sugar cube in. Have the kids count to 10 while you shake the bottle. After 10 seconds, stop and have kids look to see if the sugar cube is still there. Continue shaking the bottle, having the kids count aloud and stopping every 10 seconds to check on the progress until the sugar cube has dissolved.

Say: **The sugar cube is gone, kind of like Jesus forgave the man and made the wrong things he had done disappear. Let's see if we can make that happen more than once!**

Invite one child to try it. Help that child open the water bottle and put in a sugar cube. Make sure to replace the lid. Have the child shake the water bottle while the other children count. Have the child stop shaking it every 10 seconds to check how much the sugar cube has "disappeared."

After that sugar cube has disappeared, say: **I wonder if we can make two sugar cubes disappear.** Invite a new child to try it, this time with two sugar cubes. Follow the same process as before.

Say: **Jesus forgave the man for a lot of wrong things he did.** Give each child one sugar cube, and count the sugar cubes as you hand them out, saying, "Jesus forgave the man of one, two, three [and so on] wrong things he did."

Give each child a water bottle. Say: **Let's all make our sugar cubes disappear to show that Jesus forgave the man and made the wrong things the man had done disappear.** Lead all the children in the same process as before, but have all the children do it at once.

"Dissolve" Sins
Say: **All your sugar cubes disappeared in the water!**

Invite kids to talk about what they liked about watching the sugar cubes disappear.

Say: **Jesus forgave the man, and Jesus forgives us. Jesus made the man's sins disappear. A sin is something we do that we know is wrong—like lying about something we broke, saying something mean to a friend, or not helping Mom when she asks.**

Share about something wrong that you did when you were a child.

Show another sugar cube. Say: **I did something wrong.** Drop the sugar cube into your water bottle. **But Jesus makes it disappear. He forgives me.**

Give each child another sugar cube.

Say: **Think of something you did that was wrong. Jesus forgives you for what you did.** Have the children drop the sugar cubes into their water bottles. **Jesus makes your sins disappear. Jesus forgives you.**

Have children shake their water bottles, and lead them in a prayer, thanking Jesus that he forgives us.

A MiRACULOUS CATCH OF FiSH

Luke 5:1-11

Supplies
- white paper
- white crayons
- thick blue washable markers (1 per child)

Easy Prep
- Use a white crayon to draw at least 1 simple fish profile on a white sheet of paper. You'll need 1 of these per child. Vary how big, how many, and the location of the fish so each child's paper is unique. Draw the fish with force so the line of wax is thick—this will help the fish show up better.

MiRACULOUS FiSH APPEARANCE

What Kids Will Do
Kids discover fish on a page they color.

Reveal the Fish
Say: **The Bible tells us about some fishermen who worked hard all night but didn't catch any fish. Then Jesus got into their boat. He told them to fish again, and they caught *so* many fish! Jesus did something amazing. <u>Jesus *is* amazing</u>!**

Give each child a white sheet of paper that you prepared ahead of time, setting the pages in front of kids so the white crayon is facing up.

Say: **Let's see if we can catch any fish. I have a feeling that if we color some water on these pages, we'll see some fish, too.**

Have the children use blue markers to color over their pages until they see the fish profiles you drew ahead of time. Encourage them to color over the entire page because fish could be hidden anywhere on the page.

Jesus is amazing.

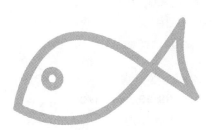

Invite each child to show off the fish he or she "caught."

Talk About It

Ask:

- **What did you think or feel when you found a fish on your page?**

Say: **It seems like the fishermen were surprised and excited, too! It was amazing that they caught so many fish! Jesus is amazing. He can do a lot of surprising and exciting things for us, too.**

If time allows, give the children white crayons and paper, and let them make secret designs on the papers. Have them trade papers and use marker to reveal the pictures.

Share one or two surprising, exciting, or amazing things Jesus has done in *your* life that helped you.

Ask:

- **What amazing things do you think Jesus can do to help *you*?**

Say: **Jesus can do anything. Jesus is amazing!**

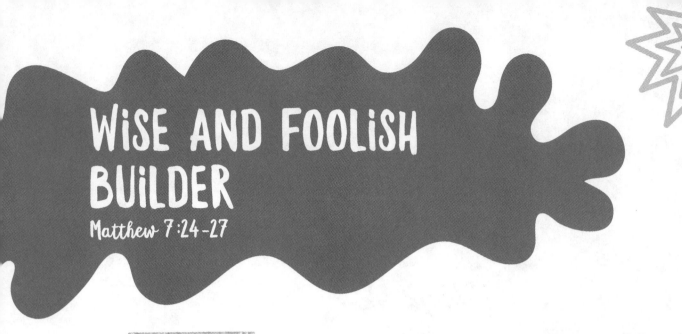

WISE AND FOOLISH BUILDER
Matthew 7:24-27

Supplies
- baking pan with sides
- foaming shaving cream
- bricks (1 for every 4 kids)
- small toy figures (1 per child)
- wet wipes
- cup of water

A SOLID FOUNDATION

What Kids Will Do
Kids set up foundations.

Set Up Two Foundations
Say: **In the Bible, Jesus tells us about the two different places where people build a house.** Place a brick on one side of the baking pan, and spray a pile of shaving cream on the other side of the pan.

Say: **Let's pretend that these are two different places to build a house.**

Invite children to tell which place seems stronger. Then invite one child to place a toy figure on the brick and another child to place a different toy figure on the pile of shaving cream. Help the children talk again about which seems stronger based on what happened.

Ask:
- **What just happened?**
- **Which place seemed stronger to build a house on?**
- **What do you think will happen if it rains here?**

Jesus is trustworthy.

After children have shared their ideas, pour water over the brick and then over the shaving cream, and talk with children about what happened.

Explore the Two Foundations

Say: **It seems like the brick is a much better place to build a house. But now it's your turn to explore which one seems better!** Spray a pile of shaving cream in front of each child, and place a brick in between every four or so children. Give each child a toy figure. Encourage children to explore the two foundations using their hands and the toy.

Talk About It

Point at a brick and a pile of shaving cream and say: **In the Bible, Jesus tells about a safe place to build a house. He said to build your house on a rock.**

Ask:

- **Why is it smart to build your house in a safe place?**

Say: **It's smart to build a house in a safe, trustworthy place because then we can trust that the house is safe and know that we'll be safe. But Jesus wasn't just talking about houses. He wants people to know that *he* is like a strong rock that we can depend on every day, too. He won't be wiggly or melt away like the shaving cream. We can have Jesus as our friend every day, and we can know that he will always be there for us and that we can trust him — because Jesus is trustworthy!**

JESUS EATS WITH SINNERS AT MATTHEW'S HOUSE

Matthew 9:9-13

Supplies
- shoebox or small cardboard box
- extra-large container, such as a plastic storage bin or large cardboard box
- classroom toys (1 per child)

TIP!

For older kids, instead of pointing out the similarities and differences, ask the kids to discuss them.

EVERY TOY CAN FIT

What Kids Will Do
Kids fit toys in a box.

Choose a Toy
Have kids sit in a circle.

Say: **Jesus came for everyone. That means he came for you and for your family. It means he came for your friends and for people you don't know. It means he came for people who are just like you and for people who are different from you.**

When I say "go," choose one toy you like in our room, and then come sit back down in our circle.

Have each child choose one toy and return to the circle. If you have a small group, encourage children to choose large toys so that the toys will not all be able to fit in the shoebox.

Point out some similarities between toys that were chosen. ("These three friends chose toys that are alike—their toys are all baby dolls.")

Jesus came for everyone.

Point out some differences between toys that were chosen. ("You chose a car, but this friend chose dress-up clothes.")

Say: **Like your toys, you are like each other in some ways and unlike each other in other ways, too.**

Try to Fit All the Toys
Hold up the shoebox.

Say: **Let's see if we can fit *all* your toys into this box.**

Have the children try to fit all the toys into the shoebox. After the children notice that all the toys can't fit in the box, say: **Hmm…well, let's see what toys we *can* make fit.**

Have kids each take back the toys they chose, and have kids put only some of the toys in the box, such as all the baby dolls or all the toys with wheels. Repeat a few times so different groups of kids can put their toys in the box.

Say: **We got *some* kinds of toys to fit in the box, but we weren't able to fit *all* the toys inside. That reminds me of a Bible story where some people thought Jesus shouldn't spend time with people who weren't like them—people they thought were different. They thought some people should be left out from Jesus' love—like how some types of toys were left out when we tried to fit them in the box. But <u>Jesus came for everyone</u>. He wants everyone to be in his family.**

Find a Box Where Every Toy Fits
Bring over the large container, and have kids put their toys inside.

Say: **Yay! All our different toys fit inside this box—every single one! This box is more like Jesus. Just like we were able to fit all the toys inside this box and none of them were left out, <u>Jesus came for everyone</u>, and he doesn't want anyone to be left out from his love. He wants every single person to be his friend!**

JESUS HEALS A LAME MAN BY A POOL

John 5:1-18

Supplies
- modeling dough
- gingerbread-man cookie cutter

SHAPE THE DOUGH

What Kids Will Do
Kids make different shapes with clay.

Make Different Shapes
Say: **The Bible says** <u>Jesus is God</u>**. That means he can do all kinds of amazing things. One time he healed a man who was lying by a pool. The man couldn't walk, but Jesus told him to get up and start walking—and he did! Let's play with some modeling dough to help us learn more about what it means that** <u>Jesus is God</u>**.**

Give each child a handful of modeling dough.

Say: **Make a pancake with your modeling dough.** Lead kids in making "pancakes," and then let the children show off what they made.

Say: **This modeling dough is in the *shape* of pancakes.**

Lead the children to make several different things, such as a ball, a baseball bat, a snake, and a bowl. Older kids can make more difficult shapes, such as a snowman, a cross, or a wristwatch. After they make each thing, remind them that the objects are modeling dough in the shape of the things they made.

Jesus is God.

Try to Shape God

Have the children use the modeling dough to try to make a shape that looks like God. Let the children work without giving them the impression that there's a right or wrong way to do it.

Invite the children to show what they made.

Say: **Today we learned that <u>Jesus is God</u>.** Lead the children to each make a person shape. You can use a gingerbread-man cookie cutter with younger children.

Say: **<u>Jesus is God</u> in the shape of a person. That means that Jesus was a person like you and me, but he's also God. When we look at Jesus, we see God because <u>Jesus is God</u>. Like how you made your modeling dough into the shape of a pancake, <u>Jesus is God</u> in the shape of a person!**

A ROMAN OFFICER DEMONSTRATES FAITH

Luke 7:1-10; Matthew 8:5-13

Supplies

- large magnets or magnetic wands (1 for every 4 children)
- metal paper clips (small box for every 4 children)
- metal cookie sheets or magnetic boards (1 for every 4 children)

TIP!

Monitor children to ensure they don't put the paper clips in their mouths.

MAGNET AUTHORITY

What Kids Will Do

Kids use magnets to move things.

Move the Magnet

Say: **The Bible says that <u>Jesus has authority over everything</u>. One time he even healed a servant just by speaking. Jesus can make anything happen. He can make waves stop moving, and he can make wind blow. He has authority over us, too. Let's try something to help us experience that.**

Pour the paper clips onto a cookie sheet or magnetic board.

Ask:

- **Do you think I can move these paper clips without touching them? How about by just commanding them to move?**

Say: **Cross your arms if you think I can't.** Demonstrate the gesture. **Make muscle arms if you think I can.** Demonstrate the gesture. **Let's find out. Let's pretend that this magnet is Jesus.** Show the magnet.

Say: **Paper clips, move over here.** Point to where you want the paper clips to move.

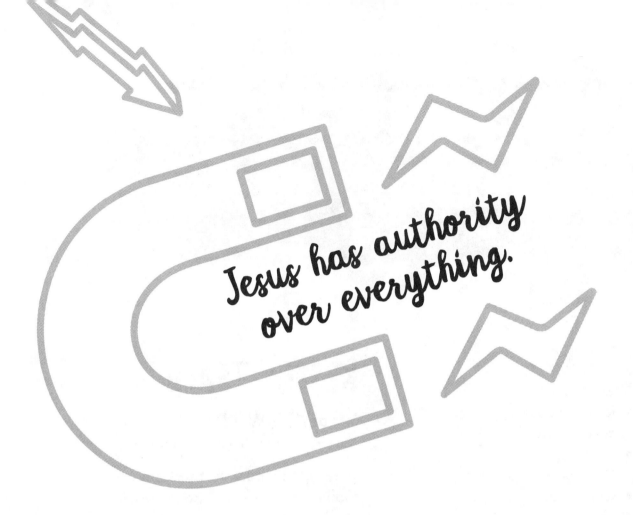

Jesus has authority over everything.

Slowly move the magnet underneath the cookie sheet. Say: **Paper clips, move over here.** Point to where you want the paper clips to move. Slowly move the magnet underneath the cookie sheet.

Ask:

- **What's happening to the paper clips?** Take a few responses.

Say: **The magnet is leading, guiding, and controlling the paper clips. Jesus' authority is kind of like that. One time in the Bible, there was a sick servant. All Jesus did was speak, and the sickness went away. Jesus has the strength and power to lead and guide you.**

Play With Magnets

Say: **It's your turn to command the paper clips. We'll take turns. One person will command where on the tray to move the paper clips and another person will use the magnet under the tray to move them. Then you'll switch so others will get a chance to play.**

Help children get into groups of four. Distribute the cookie sheets, paper clips, and magnets. Let the children take turns, encouraging them to switch so everyone gets a chance to play. Let them play as long as time allows.

Say: **Just as the magnet guided the paper clips, Jesus has the strength and power to lead and guide you. He can make anything happen in your life. <u>Jesus has authority over everything!</u>**

JESUS EASES JOHN'S DOUBT

Matthew 11:1-6; Luke 7:18-23

Supplies

- ice cube trays (for 1 ice cube for every 2 children)
- shallow pans (1 for every 4 children)
- warm water
- salt
- small toy figures (1 for every 2 children)
- cooler with ice packs
- thermos or mug of warm water (optional)

Easy Prep

- Freeze child-safe toy figures, such as child-safe Lego characters or little green army men, in water using the ice cube trays, 1 figure per section. Place the ice cubes in a cooler with ice packs. If you don't have a faucet with warm water available, bring warm water in a thermos or mug.

RESCUE TEAM!

What Kids Will Do

Kids rescue toy figures from ice.

Attempt to Rescue the Icemen

Gather four children around each shallow pan.

Say: **Jesus is the Messiah. That means Jesus rescues us. He's our hero because he saves us from the most dangerous and scary things. I'll show you what I mean.**

Put two ice cubes/icemen in each pan.

Say: **These men are frozen inside the ice! How can we rescue them?** Let the children come up with ideas without helping them. Have the children work in pairs to try each idea suggested.

Kids may or may not come up with ideas that work to completely free the toy figures. If they don't, then let them use the salt and/ or warm water to work the figures free.

Talk About It

Say: **We rescued our toys! Now they're free. They can move around because they're**

Jesus is the Messiah.

not frozen anymore. Jesus frees us, too, when he rescues us. One time in the Bible, one of Jesus' friends asked him if he was really the Messiah. Jesus told his friend, "Yes, I am." He also shared about some of the ways he was rescuing people.

Share a couple of child-friendly things that Jesus, as the Messiah, can rescue you from. For example, Jesus rescues us when he helps us not be afraid in scary times, and he rescues us when he reminds us to make good choices in life.

Ask:

• **What can Jesus rescue *you* from?**

Share ways kids are free when Jesus rescues them. For example, we can stop being scared when Jesus rescues us. We can also be free from getting in trouble when Jesus rescues us from making bad choices.

Say: **Like we rescued the toys from the ice, Jesus rescues us. That's because Jesus is the Messiah.**

PARABLE OF THE FARMER AND THE SEED

Matthew 13:1-9, 18-23; Luke 8:4-15

Supplies
- paper-wrapped straws (1 per child, plus 1 for each leader)
- medicine droppers (available in the pharmacy section at discount stores or at craft and hobby stores) (1 for every 6 kids)
- cups of water
- towels for cleanup

Easy Prep
- To make the "worms" for this activity, begin by tearing off the end of the paper wrapper at one end of a straw. Carefully scrunch the wrapper down toward the other end of the straw, as if you were going to remove it. Keep the paper on the straw until the whole wrapper is fully compact on one end of the straw. Once you start scrunching the paper down, don't pull it back up, and make sure the paper doesn't get wet. Once it's fully compact, push the paper off the straw, avoiding wet surfaces. Make one worm for each child.
- Practice "growing" a couple of worms beforehand so you know how it works best. You can watch a video tutorial at ww2.group.com/reproducibles.

GROWING WORMS

What Kids Will Do
Kids grow paper worms.

Grow the Paper Worms
Say: **In the Bible, Jesus told a story about some seeds. Some of the seeds were put in places where they could grow. Others were put in places where they couldn't grow. Jesus told the story to help us learn something else. He wanted us to learn that he's the one who grows us. Jesus grows us from little babies to grown-ups, and he helps our hearts grow, too, so we can be more like him. Let's do something to help us think about that.**

Put the children into groups of six, and have each group sit in a circle. Place a paper worm in the center of each circle, and remind children not to touch it.

Show kids your paper worm. Say: **Let's pretend this is a little**

Jesus grows us.

worm. **I can make it grow!** Have adult or teen helpers do the following with each group as you demonstrate. Use a medicine dropper to drop only one drop of water onto the end of the worm. It will "grow." Continue slowly adding drops along the worm until it stops growing. The water causes the paper to "unscrunch," making it look like it's growing.

Let each child take a turn growing a worm. Have an adult or teen helper assist the children in each group to drop the water so that kids' worms grow at least a little bit. Before each child's turn, ask the children to talk about whether they think the next worm will grow longer or shorter than the last, and have them use their hands to estimate the length.

Talk About It

Ask:

- **What did you like about the growing worms?**

Say: **Some of the worms grew really well, and others didn't grow quite as well. That's like Jesus' story about the seeds. Some grew well, and others didn't. Like the worms and the seeds that grew really well, we can grow really well when <u>Jesus grows us.</u>**

Share something you like about knowing that Jesus grows you.

Ask:

- **What do you like about knowing that Jesus can grow you?**

Say: **<u>Jesus grows us</u> in really exciting ways! And he grows us really well!**

JESUS DESCRIBES HIS TRUE FAMILY

Matthew 12:46-50; Mark 3:31-35; Luke 8:19-21

Supplies
- crayons
- card stock
- newspapers or old magazines
- hair dryer
- tape

Easy Prep
- Hang the card stock on the wall within reach of kids just above some newspapers or old magazines. Make sure the newspapers or magazines are laid strategically underneath the card stock so they will catch any dripping crayon wax. Make sure the card stock is near an electrical outlet so the hair dryer can reach the card stock.
- If you have a group larger than 10 kids, hang several sheets of card stock or use a poster board.

COLOR COMBINATIONS

What Kids Will Do

Kids learn how colors combine when crayons are melted.

Choose a Color

Say: **Jesus wants us in his family. One time when Jesus was talking to a crowd of people, someone told him his mother and brothers were standing outside wanting to talk to him. But Jesus wanted everyone to know that he wanted all the people in the world to be part of his family. He wants you to be in his family, too. He loves each of you and thinks you're very special.**

Share something that's special about *you*.

Ask:
- **What's special about *you*?** Help children think of ways they're special, if needed.

Say: **Jesus thinks you're all very special, and so do I! One thing that's special about us is our favorite color.**

Jesus wants us in his family.

Have each child choose his or her favorite color crayon and gather around the card stock you hung on the wall.

Say: **Each of you found a special color. Even if you found a color that looks the same as someone else's, your crayon is special.** Point out some differences between two crayons of the same color. For example, they may be a slightly different shade, shape, or brand. **Each of you is special, like the crayon you chose.**

Take each child's crayon, and as you do, say: **This is** [name]'s **special crayon.** Then tape it, tip pointing down, to the card stock. Tape all the kids' crayons in a line next to each other (but not quite touching), making sure all the tips are pointing down.

Melt the Crayons

Say: **You're all special and unique like these crayons.** *Unique* **means there's no one who's exactly like you! Jesus wants each of you in his family. And when we're part of Jesus' family, he brings us** together like this. Turn on the hair dryer and blow hot air on the crayons. Show kids how to do it, and help them take turns holding the hair dryer. (Make sure kids keep their hands and feet at least a foot away from the hot crayon wax and the heat of the dryer.) The crayons will start dripping, and the colors will run down the paper mixing all the colors together.

Say: **All our crayons were separate** [point to the individual crayons]**, but the hair dryer melted all the colors together.** Point to the colors on the paper. **Jesus brings us all together into a family. He makes something beautiful when we're all together. He doesn't want us to be separate like these crayons.** Point to the crayons taped in a line. **He wants us all together in a family like these colors.** Point to the colors melted over the paper. **These colors are still special, but they're more beautiful all together. Jesus wants us all in his family together.**

JESUS CALMS THE STORM

Matthew 8:23-27; Mark 4:35-41; Luke 8:22-25

Supplies

- empty 2-liter bottles (2 for every 10 children)
- duct tape or Tornado Tubes (available at hobby and education stores or online at Walmart and Amazon) (1 tube for every 10 children)
- water
- glitter (optional)
- food coloring (optional)

Easy Prep

- Fill one 2-liter bottle with water. If you have it, add glitter and/ or food coloring to give the water some color and sparkle. Connect the empty 2-liter bottle to the full bottle using the Tornado Tube, or connect the 2 bottles at their openings by tightly wrapping several layers of duct tape around the mouths of the bottles. Make 1 set of connected bottles for every 10 children in your class. (Although duct tape works, you'll have a stronger connection between the bottles if you use a Tornado Tube.)

CALM THE STORM

What Kids Will Do

Kids make a tornado in a bottle.

Make Storms in a Bottle

Have children get into groups of 10, each with an adult or teen helper. Give each group one set of two connected bottles.

Say: **One time in the Bible, Jesus did something really amazing! He was with some of his friends in a boat when a scary storm started rocking the boat. Jesus' friends were so scared. But Jesus made the storm stop just by saying, "Silence! Be still!" Jesus has the power to calm storms!**

Show one set of connected bottles. Say: **I can make a storm inside these bottles, and we can watch it stop— just like Jesus stopped the storm in the Bible.**

Do the following, and have adult or teen helpers in other groups of 10 do the same: Flip the bottles over so the empty one is on the bottom. Always keep a strong hold on the bottle that's upside down. (If your bottles are taped together, hold the bottle openings to keep that connection strong.) As much as possible, keep the bottom bottle in one place while gently circling the top bottle to create a swirling motion with the water as it funnels into the bottom bottle.

Create this tornado a few times while children watch. Point out how the storm in the top turns into calm water in the bottom.

Help the children as they take turns making storms in the bottles. (The adult or teen helper can help flip the bottle for the child and then hold it in place with one hand. With the other hand, he or she can help the child make a circling motion with the top bottle.) As children take turns, help all of them talk about what they like about watching the water change. Continue to let children take turns as time allows.

Talk About It

Say: **We watched the storms in the bottles become calm like the storm that Jesus calmed for his friends. Our bottles just had tiny storms in them, but Jesus has the power to calm the big storms outside! Jesus can do anything. Jesus is amazing!**

Share some things that Jesus can do for the children, and then invite them to talk about things they think Jesus is powerful enough to do.

Say: **Thanks for sharing all those great ideas! This week, if you see a storm, remember that Jesus has so much power that he can make it stop! If he can do that, think of all the other things Jesus can do for you!**

Jesus has power to calm storms

JESUS HEALS A BLEEDING WOMAN AND RESTORES A GIRL TO LIFE

Mark 5:21-43; Matthew 9:18-26; Luke 8:40-56

Supplies

- inflated balloons (1 per child)
- small squares of paper
- confetti
- glitter
- tissue paper pieces
- pepper
- Sweet'N Low artificial sweetener
- newspapers or a plastic tablecloth

Easy Prep

- Use newspapers or a plastic tablecloth to cover your work surface for easy cleanup.

POWERFUL BALLOONS

What Kids Will Do

Kids try to pick up various items with the static on balloons.

Experiment With Balloons

Say: **Jesus has power over sickness and death! The Bible says he even stopped people from being sick when he touched them! One woman touched his clothes and she stopped being sick. Another girl had died, but when Jesus touched her, she came back to life. Let's do something to help us think about what it means that Jesus has power over sickness and death.**

Rub an inflated balloon on your clothes or hair, and show children that the balloon can now stick to your clothes or hair. If you have long hair, you can also show the children how the balloon makes your hair stick out.

Give each child a balloon, and help kids copy what you did.

TIP!

If any balloons pop, immediately pick up the pieces and throw them away.

Jesus has power over sickness and death.

Say: **That's pretty amazing—like Jesus! We can use the balloons to do a lot of things just by touching them to different things.** Lead the children in experimenting with the balloons to see what happens when they touch the balloons to each of the supplies (small squares of paper, confetti, glitter, tissue paper pieces, pepper, and the Sweet'N Low). Let each child have a turn to see what happens when his or her balloon touches that supply. Periodically remind kids to rub their balloons against their hair or clothes so they'll have more static.

If time allows, let children see what the balloons will do with other items around your room.

Talk About It

Say: **These balloons seem powerful! Just by touching them to things, they can do pretty neat stuff! Jesus is even more powerful than these balloons. When he touched people with his hand, they stopped being sick, and sometimes they came back to life! Jesus has power over sickness and death.**

JESUS WALKS ON WATER

Matthew 14:22-33; Mark 6:45-52; John 6:16-21

Supplies
- extra-large clear plastic container filled with water
- 2 oranges
- inflated item
- large rock
- variety of classroom items

Easy Prep
- Peel 1 orange.

SINK OR FLOAT

What Kids Will Do
Kids experiment with items to see if they sink.

Check Which Items Sink and Float
Say: **Did you know Jesus could walk on water? One time he also helped his friend Peter walk on the water! But Peter started getting scared, and then he started to sink!** Invite children to talk about whether they sink or float in water. **Let's play with some things to see if they sink or float in the water.**

Show the unpeeled orange. Have kids vote whether they think it will sink or float. Choose one child to drop it into the container while everyone watches what happens.

Say: **I guess oranges float!** Show the peeled orange. **But this orange is peeled. Do you think it'll float, too?** Have kids vote whether they think it will sink or float. Choose one child to drop it into the container while everyone watches what happens.

Jesus calms our fears.

Say: **That was tricky! One orange floated, but the other didn't.** Show the inflated item, and have kids vote whether they think it will sink or float. Choose one child to drop it into the container while everyone watches what happens.

Show the rock, and have kids vote whether they think it will sink or float. Choose one child to drop it into the container while everyone watches what happens.

Say: **What about things around our room?** Let kids suggest things around the room to test in the water. Choose items you're okay with getting wet, and then let the children retrieve them. For each item, have kids vote, and then test to see if it floats.

Talk About It

Say: **With Jesus' help, Peter could walk on the water, kind of like how some of our items floated in the tub of water. But when Peter got scared, he started to sink. Peter didn't need to be scared because Jesus was there with him. Jesus helped Peter back into the boat and calmed his fears. Jesus is with us, too, and <u>he calms our fears</u>.**

JESUS IS TRANSFIGURED

Matthew 17:1-13; Mark 9:2-13; Luke 9:28-36

Supplies

- highlighter
- needle-nose pliers
- empty clear plastic bottle with a lid
- hydrogen peroxide
- water
- smartphone or flashlight
- large box (optional)

Easy Prep

- Fill the bottle halfway with water. Add hydrogen peroxide so the bottle is about ¾ full. Put the bottle out of children's reach.
- If you can't get your room very dark, you can place the bottle inside a large box turned on its side so children will be able to see the same effect.

GLOWING BOTTLE

What Kids Will Do
Kids help make a glowing bottle.

Share About Surprising Events
Say: **One time Jesus and his friends climbed a mountain. When they were at the top, Jesus' friends saw God change the way Jesus looked—God made Jesus' face glow like the sun. God told Jesus' friends that Jesus is his special Son whom he loves. Jesus' friends were really surprised to see Jesus change like he did. It amazed them!**

Share about something amazing that would surprise *you*. What you share doesn't have to be realistic.

Ask:

- **Tell about something amazing that would surprise *you*.** Help the children think of ideas. They might be amazed by seeing lightning or a rainbow in the sky. It's okay if they share make-believe things. The idea is to help them think of things that are amazing to them.

Change the Appearance of the Water
Say: **The Bible says that the way Jesus**

Jesus is God.

looked changed! It really happened right in front of Jesus' friends. That must've been really surprising. I have something pretty cool to show you like that.

Show the bottle, and then darken the room. Say: **We're going to make this bottle change so it glows, kind of like Jesus glowed.** Use the needle-nose pliers to pull the highlighter pad from inside the highlighter. (Avoid touching the highlighter with your hands because it could stain.) Place it in the bottle, and replace the bottle lid.

Have children take turns shaking the bottle. After about a minute, turn on your smartphone's light or the flashlight, and place the bottle on it. The bottle will begin to glow as the highlighter mixes into the liquid. The more the children shake it, the faster and better it will work.

Allow time for children to observe it.

Talk About It
Ask:
• **What do you think about what happened?** Help the children talk

about it by starting with something you liked about the glowing bottle.

Say: **This was just some water that changed colors, and I used a light to make it glow. But Jesus *really* glowed. His face was bright like the sun! His clothes even glowed. God made him glow like that. God wanted us to know that Jesus is really special.**

Ask:
• **What do you think about Jesus changing like that?**

Say: **What happened showed Jesus' friends that <u>Jesus is God</u>. God even talked to Jesus' friends right there. He told them that he loves Jesus! We can love Jesus, too, and we can believe that <u>Jesus is God</u>.**

PARABLE OF THE GOOD SAMARITAN

Luke 10:25-37

Supplies
- water (1½ cups)
- liquid dish soap (½ cup)
- corn syrup (at least ½ cup)
- medium bowl
- spoon
- bubble wand or chenille wire
- trash bags

Easy Prep
- If you don't have a bubble wand, make 1 with a chenille wire by forming a loop with the end of the chenille wire and twisting the end around the straight part.
- Mix water, liquid dish soap, and corn syrup in a bowl. Use the bubble wand to test how strong your bubbles are. You'll want them to be strong enough that you can catch 1 and hold it for 20 seconds to a minute. (Prepare this mixture just before class to ensure the corn syrup retains its stickiness that keeps the bubbles from popping easily.)
- This bubble solution will wash off skin and clothes, but it's harder to clean from carpet because of the sticky corn syrup. If possible, do this activity in an area without carpet, or cut open trash bags and place them over carpets and upholstery for easy cleanup.

CARE FOR THE BUBBLES

What Kids Will Do
Kids play gently with bubbles.

Play With Bubbles
Say: **Jesus told a story about some people who walked right by someone who was hurt and didn't stop to help. But there was one man who *did* stop to help. Sometimes we call that man "the good Samaritan" because he cared for the hurt person beside the road. Jesus says we can care for others, too. Let's play a game to help us practice caring for something.**

Blow bubbles from your homemade solution, and encourage children to catch them and "care" for them by trying to keep them safe. They can hold them carefully and try to keep them from breaking. You can

Jesus-followers care for others.

let older kids take turns blowing the bubbles, too. Play as time allows.

Talk About It

Ask:

- **What did you do to keep the bubbles safe and cared for?**

Say: **You all did a great job caring for the bubbles! It was good practice for caring for our friends and families. And that's what we do when Jesus is our friend! The Bible says that Jesus-followers care for others. You can care for others by being kind and gentle like you were with the bubbles.**

JESUS FEEDS FIVE THOUSAND

Matthew 14:13-21; Mark 6:30-44; Luke 9:10-17; John 6:1-15

Supplies
- magnifying glasses (at least 1 for every 4 kids)

Easy Prep
- This activity will work better if you use higher-quality magnifying glasses. If you don't want to buy new magnifying glasses, consider borrowing some from local classrooms or individuals in your church.

SEEING THE UNEXPECTED

What Kids Will Do
Kids look for surprising things about classroom objects.

Look Through a Magnifying Glass
Say: **The Bible says that <u>Jesus does the unexpected</u>. He does things that surprise us. One time he was speaking to a group of 5,000 people and everyone started to get hungry. There wasn't very much food, but Jesus made the food multiply. Because he's God, he could make it so there was enough food for all the people. What he did was a surprise to everyone! Let's use some magnifying glasses to see some things that might surprise us. Magnifying glasses help us see things in a new way.**

Have kids find a toy or other item in the room to hold. Then help children form groups of four and sit on the floor with the items they found.

Say: **First, let's look at the things we found without magnifying glasses.**

Jesus does the unexpected.

Lead kids to look at and talk about the size, shape, color, and texture of the things they found.

Then give each group a magnifying glass, and say: **Now let's look at the things we found through the magnifying glasses.** Show young kids how to hold the magnifying glasses so they can look more closely at the things they found. Help children talk about how the things they found might look different through their magnifying glasses. For example, ask them if the colors look different at all. Can they see any dust that they couldn't see before? If there are bumps on their objects, do the bumps look bigger through the magnifying glasses?

Talk About It

Gather the magnifying glasses, and ask:

- **What surprised you when you looked through your magnifying glass?** Start the sharing by looking through a magnifying glass and sharing something *you* saw that was surprising or interesting.

Say: **Maybe you saw something that surprised you—something you didn't expect! Maybe you saw some little lines or bumps, or you saw some dust you didn't see before. Those things were surprising and unexpected. Jesus' friends saw Jesus do something that surprised them! They saw him feed a lot of people with just a little bit of food. Jesus can do surprising things for you, too. He can do surprising things to take care of you, just like he fed all those people in a surprising way.**

Tell a few ways that Jesus takes care of *you*. Preferably, give examples of ways that were surprising.

Ask:

- **What are some ways Jesus can take care of *you*?**

Say: **Jesus always takes care of us! And sometimes <u>he does the unexpected</u> to take care of us. Jesus is amazing!**

65

DISCIPLES ARGUE ABOUT WHO WILL BE THE GREATEST

Matthew 18:1-6; Mark 9:33-37; Luke 9:46-48

Supplies
- toothpicks (1 per child)
- packing peanuts (1 per child)

Easy Prep
- Make a square, a cross, and a triangle out of no more than 4 toothpicks and 4 packing peanuts for each shape.

Jesus shows us what it means to be great.

BUILDING TOGETHER

What Kids Will Do
Kids build shapes with packing peanuts and toothpicks.

Build Shapes
Say: **The Bible says one time Jesus' friends were arguing about who was the greatest. But Jesus surprised them by explaining that when we serve others, it makes us great. That wasn't just for Jesus' friends—Jesus says we're great when we serve others, too. And we want to be great because we want to be like Jesus, who loves us so much.**

One way we can serve others is by working together and helping each other. Hold up a toothpick and packing peanut. **I'm going to give each of you a toothpick and a packing peanut. Let's see if we can work together and use our toothpicks and packing peanuts to build some fun shapes.**

Help kids form groups of four and sit on the floor. Then give each child a toothpick and a packing peanut.

Say: **You each have a toothpick and a packing peanut. But you won't be able to**

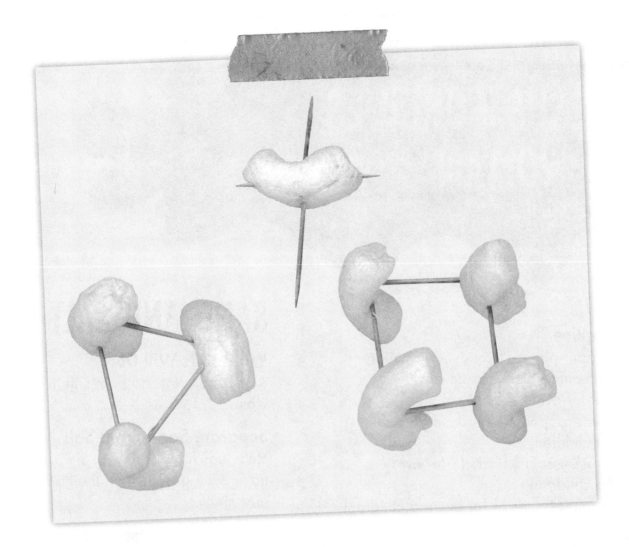

build anything by yourself. So let's work together and see what we can build!

One at a time, hold up the shapes you made beforehand and help kids work together to make those shapes. Have adult or teen helpers work with each group of four. Make sure kids are each contributing at least one of their items to build each shape.

Gather the toothpicks and packing peanuts when you've finished.

Talk About It
Say: **You did a great job working together to make your shapes!**

Ask:

• **What did *you* like about working together?** Start the discussion by telling kids something *you* like about working together with others.

Say: **Each of you helped by sharing your toothpicks and packing peanuts. And no one person's pieces were more important than any of the others. That's what <u>Jesus showed his friends about what it means to be great</u>. Jesus says we're great when we share and help each other.**

JESUS FORGIVES A WOMAN

John 8:1-11

Supplies

- paper plates (1 for every 6 children)
- 16-ounce clear plastic cups (2 for every 6 children)
- plastic spoons (3 for every 6 children)
- basket coffee filters (1 for every 6 children)
- rubber bands (1 for every 6 children)
- paper towels
- salt
- sand
- water
- ¼-teaspoon measuring spoon

Easy Prep

- Beforehand, mix together ¼ teaspoon of sand and ¼ teaspoon of salt for every 6 children. Place each mixture on separate paper plates.
- Fill half the plastic cups about ½ full of water. Insert a coffee filter about 1½ inches into each of the remaining cups. Fold the edges of the coffee filters over the rims of the cups and secure them by placing rubber bands around the tops of the cups.

SAND AND SALT

What Kids Will Do

Kids separate sand from salt in water.

Separate Sand From Salt

Help kids form groups of six, and have each group sit on the floor in a circle.

Give the adult or teen helper in each group one paper plate with the sand and salt mixture, one cup with water, one cup with a coffee filter, three plastic spoons, and several paper towels in case there's a spill.

Say: **When we make bad choices, it makes our hearts sad. We can't make our hearts better by ourselves. Only Jesus can do that when Jesus forgives us. It's something only Jesus does.**

Hold up a paper plate with the sand and salt mixture, and say: **Let's do something to help us understand that only Jesus can fix our hearts. Your group has a** plate with some sand and salt on it. The sand and salt are mixed together. Let's try to take all the sand away from the salt with our fingers. Have the children in each group see if they can separate the sand and salt by playing in it with their fingers.

After children have had time to play with the sand and salt mixture, say: Taking the sand away with our fingers isn't working very well, so let's try something different. Let's put the sand and salt in some water and see if that helps.

Have the adult or teen helpers in each group carefully pour the sand and salt from the plate into the cup of water as kids watch. Then have kids take turns trying to get the sand out of the water with spoons. If children happen to get any sand out of the water, have them put the sand on the paper plates.

Say: Putting the sand and salt in water didn't help much. Even though you can't see the salt anymore, it's still there. And the sand and salt are still mixed together in the water. So let's try one more thing. Let's pour the water through the papers in the other cups and see what happens.

Have the adult or teen helpers stir the water with a spoon and then slowly pour the water into the cups with the filters. As the sand collects in the filters, the helpers may have to slightly tip the cups in different directions to help the last of the water go through. After all the water has gone through the filters, have

Jesus forgives.

the helpers carefully remove the rubber bands from the cups. Then have them take the filters out of the cups—without spilling any of the sand—and drop the filters into the empty cups so they won't make a mess.

Let children look at the water in the cup to see what happened to the sand.

Talk About It
Ask:

- **What surprised you about this experiment?**

Say: We couldn't take all the sand away on our own, no matter how hard we tried. But when the water went through the papers, the salt stayed in the water and the sand came out. That's like what Jesus does for us when he forgives us. The Bible tells about a time some people wanted to hurt a woman for the wrong things she did, but Jesus reminded them that they had done wrong things, too. He showed everyone that he's the one who can forgive us for the wrong things we do. He takes away our sins just like the papers took the sand away from the salt in the water.

JESUS VISITS MARY AND MARTHA

Luke 10:38-42

Supplies

- glass drinking glasses (2 for every 6 children)
- metal spoons (1 for every 6 children)
- water

Easy Prep

- Fill each glass about ½ full of water.

SINGING GLASSES

What Kids Will Do

Kids listen to sounds made by tapping drinking glasses.

Listen to the Sounds of Glasses

Help kids form groups of six and sit in a circle.

Give each group two glasses of water and one metal spoon.

Say: **The Bible says that Jesus wants to be our friend. One thing Jesus taught his friends Mary and Martha is that friends listen to each other. Let's practice our listening.**

Let children take turns gently tapping the glasses of water with a metal spoon.

Ask:

- **Explain whether you think the glasses sound the same or not.**

Say: **Let's change the amount of water in the glasses and find out if the sound changes.**

In each group, have an adult or teen helper pour about half the water from one glass into the other glass.

Jesus wants to be our friend.

Ask:

- **What do you think the glasses will sound like now?**

Let children take turns gently tapping the glasses again with the metal spoon.

Talk About It

Let the children share their reactions, and then ask:

- **What did you have to do to tell how the glasses sounded?**

Say: **In the same way we listened to the sound the glasses made, friends listen to each other. In the Bible story I mentioned earlier, Mary listened to Jesus. Jesus liked that, and Jesus likes it when we listen to him because <u>Jesus wants to be</u> <u>our friend.</u> Like we listen to Jesus, he listens to us, too, when we pray.**

If you have extra time, lead all the groups in making up a song with their glasses. Have a child in each group tap one of the group's glasses one time whenever you point to that group. Then have that child give the spoon to another child in his or her group to tap on a glass the next time you point to that group. Make sure as many children as possible have a turn tapping a glass. The song kids play doesn't have to be a recognizable tune.

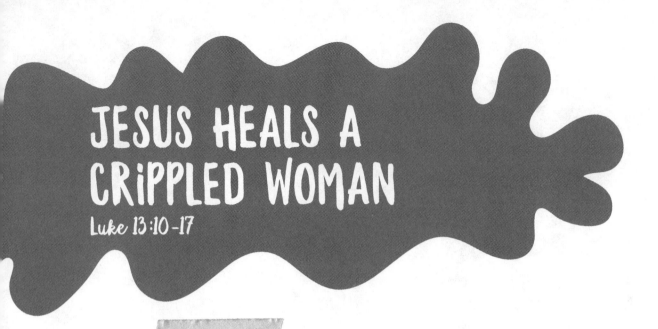

JESUS HEALS A CRIPPLED WOMAN

Luke 13:10-17

Supplies
- aluminum foil
- pennies (about 5 per child)
- large plastic containers (1 for every 4-5 children)

Easy Prep
- Cut a 6x6-inch piece of aluminum foil for every child, plus a few extras in case some tear or get completely crumpled.
- Fill each plastic container with about 2 inches of water.

Jesus does what's right—no matter what.

ALWAYS AFLOAT

What Kids Will Do
Kids make aluminum-foil boats.

Make Aluminum Foil Float
Spread out the plastic containers of water on the floor.

Have kids sit around the plastic containers in groups of about four.

Give each child a piece of aluminum foil, and tell kids not to crumple it.

Say: **The Bible says that <u>Jesus does what's right—no matter what</u>. That means he does the right thing all the time. One time Jesus went to a place like church and met a woman there who was hunched over. He healed her so she could stand up straight again. Some leaders didn't like that Jesus healed the woman because they had some rules that said people couldn't do any work on that special day. But Jesus does the right thing all the time, so even though it was a special day, he healed her anyway.**

Let's do something to think about how <u>Jesus does what's right—no matter what</u>.

We'll see if we can make our foil pieces float *all the time*. Make your foil piece into a shape you think will float. You can make a cup or a boat, or you can even leave it flat.

Have adult or teen helpers assist children in shaping their aluminum foil into something children think will float.

Let children put their aluminum-foil shapes in the water to see what happens. Make sure every child has a piece of foil that is floating. If a child gets too much water on the top and it sinks, give the child a new piece of foil.

TIP!

When we tested this idea, we discovered that even a completely flat piece of aluminum foil will hold almost 30 coins before sinking. As long as the shape doesn't allow water to flow on top of the foil, any shape will hold kids' coins.

Say: **Let's see if our foil pieces will still float if we put something on top of them.**

Give each child five pennies. Remind children not to put the pennies in their mouths. Have each child place one penny onto the aluminum foil to see if it

still floats. Then have children add the other pennies one at a time.

As time allows, let children change the shapes of their foil pieces and try the experiment again. Collect the pennies, and put them out of reach of the children.

TIP!

Watch young kids closely to ensure they don't put the pennies in their mouths.

Talk About It
Ask:

• **What surprised you about the aluminum-foil shapes?**

Say: **When you put your foil shapes in the water, they floated. They even floated after you put the pennies on them. In the same way, nothing can push Jesus down. <u>Jesus always does what's right</u>. Nothing can keep Jesus from doing the right thing.**

JESUS HEALS A BLIND MAN
John 9:1-41

Supplies
- inflated balloons (1 per child, plus a few extra)

TIP!

If a child's balloon pops, immediately pick up the pieces and throw them away. Then give that child a new balloon to use.

UNSEEN POWER

What Kids Will Do
Kids play with balloons to see the power of static electricity.

Create Static Electricity With Balloons
Gather kids, and have them sit on the floor.

Say: **The Bible says** <u>Jesus has the power to heal</u>**. We can't see the power, but we can see what it does—like in the Bible when Jesus used mud and his spit to heal a blind man. The people couldn't see Jesus' power, but they saw what his power could do. Let's do something to help us understand how we can see Jesus' power at work.**

Give each child a balloon, and show kids how to rub the balloons on their clothes to create static electricity.

Have adult or teen helpers show children how to hold their balloons close to their skin without touching it. Ask if they can feel a difference when they bring the balloons close to their skin. Explain that what they're feeling is called *static electricity*.

Jesus has the power to heal.

Then have children experiment with trying to stick the balloons to the walls or to their clothes. They can also see if the balloons will stick to other things in the room.

Finally, have children use the balloons to make their hair—or the hair of a friend—move.

Periodically remind children to rub their balloons against their clothes again to create more static.

Let kids experiment as time allows.

Talk About It

Ask:

- **What surprised you about the balloons?**

Say: **Rubbing the balloons on your clothes gave the balloons power. You couldn't see the power, but you could feel it on your skin and you could see what it did. In the same way, we can't see Jesus' healing power, but we know it's there. We can see what Jesus' power does when he uses it to help people.**

JESUS CLAIMS TO BE GOD'S SON

John 10:22-42

Supplies

- 16-ounce box of cornstarch
- measuring cup
- water
- disposable aluminum pie tin
- newspaper or plastic tablecloth
- "solid" object, such as a block or classroom toy
- small, clear container partially filled with water
- wet wipes or paper towels and water to clean hands

Jesus is God's Son.

Easy Prep

- Lay out newspapers or a plastic tablecloth, and set the disposable pie tin on top. Measure 1 cup of cornstarch into the pie tin, add ½ cup of water, and mix with your hands until well blended. Then add an additional cup of cornstarch and ½ cup water, and continue to mix until blended. The cornstarch mixture can be made up to 1 day in advance and stored in a resealable plastic bag (no refrigeration needed), but it will need to be remixed right before the lesson as it will have separated some.

- If you have more than 6 to 8 children in your class, you may want to make multiple batches of the cornstarch mixture so that every child can have a turn to experience and play with the cornstarch. Kids love playing with it!

- Test the mixture, and continue slowly adding very small amounts of either ingredient until it reaches the consistency of thick pancake batter. You should be able to form the mixture into a "solid" ball as you roll it between your hands, and then when you stop rolling, the mixture will flow like a liquid through your hands.

THE SOLID LIQUID

What Kids Will Do

Kids experiment with a mixture that's both a solid and a liquid.

Experiment With the Cornstarch

Say: **I have something really cool for us to play with today!** Show kids the cornstarch mixture. **Do you think this stuff is a solid** (hold up the "solid" object) **like this** [object] **that's hard and stays the same shape even when I squeeze it? Or do you think it's liquid** (hold up the container of water and swirl it around) **like this water that moves and swirls and splashes?**

Ask:

- **So what do you think? Do you think this goop is a solid or a liquid?** Allow kids to guess.

Say: **Let's find out!** Lightly smack or press your hand down on the substance, and point out that it doesn't splash or move around. Explain that it's kind of like a solid.

Then roll some of the mixture between your hands into a ball before holding your hand flat and allowing the mixture to flow over your hand and back into the pan. Tell children that now it is acting like a liquid by flowing and moving and changing shape.

Say: **Wow, this is so neat!**

Ask:

- **What surprised you about this stuff?**

Say: **This goop acts like a solid** *and* **a liquid. It's both things at the same time! That reminds me of what Jesus said in the Bible. He said** he's God's Son. **When Jesus was on earth, he was a person like all of us. But Jesus is also God's very special Son! He's two things at the same time—a man and God's special Son!**

With the time remaining, allow each child to experiment with the cornstarch mixture. An easy way to do this is to hand a child a rolled-up "ball" and tell him or her to keep rolling it before stopping and allowing it to flow back into the pan. Make sure children stay over the newspaper or plastic tablecloth to keep cleanup easy. After kids have each had a turn, help clean their hands.

Say: **Like this fun stuff we played with that's a solid and a liquid, Jesus is a man** *and* he's God's Son. **He's two things at the same time!**

TIP!

After the lesson, dispose of the cornstarch mixture by putting it in the trash. **Do not** pour it down a sink, as it will clog the pipes.

PARABLES OF THE LOST SHEEP AND LOST COIN

Luke 15:1-10

Supplies

- child-safe magnets (1 for every 6 kids) (see Tip below)
- small metal objects, such as washers, large paper clips, or coins
- shallow tubs filled with packing peanuts or cotton balls (1 tub for every 6 kids)

Easy Prep

- Place several metal objects in each tub, making sure the objects are mostly hidden from view. You can provide 2 or 3 magnets for every group of 6 and have children take turns searching for the hidden metal objects.

MAGNETIC SEARCH

What Kids Will Do

Kids experiment with magnets.

Use Magnets to Search for Hidden Objects

Say: **One time Jesus told a couple of stories to help his friends know that he loves them and wants to protect them. In one of the stories, Jesus told how a man lost one of his sheep and then left all his other sheep to go looking for it. He also told about a woman who lost some money and then looked everywhere to try to find it. When she found it, she was so excited that she had a party. Jesus told these stories to let us know that <u>he looks for us</u>, too. He doesn't want us to be lost. He wants us to be safe, so he'll always look for us. Let's play with something that looks for hidden things.**

TIP! → Child-safe magnets are those that are too large for kids to swallow and aren't super magnets.

Jesus looks for us.

Organize kids into groups of no more than six, and give each group a tub and several magnets. Have kids take turns moving the magnets through the tub to see what the magnets find. After a few minutes, have kids switch places so that others can have a turn. While kids are experimenting, have them talk about places they look when they lose something, such as under the bed or in between couch cushions.

Talk About It

Once everyone has had a turn, hold up some of the metal objects kids found in the tubs, and say: **The magnets helped us find all the metal objects in the tubs—all the things that are silver and shiny and hard. Magnets look especially for things that are metal. Even if those metal things are hiding and there is a lot of stuff in the way, a magnet can find** **them! And Jesus always knows where we are, too, because** <u>**Jesus looks for us**</u> **and loves us so much! Just like nothing could get in the way of the magnets finding the metal, nothing can get in the way of Jesus' love for us!**

Be aware that small objects can be a choking hazard to younger children. Remind kids not to put anything in their mouths during this activity, and have one adult or teen helper supervising each group of children.

PARABLE OF THE PRODIGAL SON

Luke 15:11-32

Supplies

- tall, clear glasses (1 for every 8 kids)
- raisins (1 per child, plus extras)
- salt
- baking sheet
- access to an oven
- clear soda

Easy Prep

- Place the raisins on a baking sheet. Sprinkle them with salt, and then bake at 200 degrees for 5 minutes. We tried this experiment many ways, and the results were not consistent without baking the raisins. We recommend you follow the baking instructions and then test a few raisins to ensure they perform as expected. If they don't, try baking them for another couple of minutes.

RISING RAISINS

What Kids Will Do

Kids watch raisins dance in clear soda.

Talk About Choices

Gather children in a circle. Fill each glass with clear soda, and set the glasses near you.

Say: **One time Jesus told a story about a son who took his dad's money and left home. He made some bad choices, but then he came back to his dad and his dad forgave him! Let's think about some bad choices kids might make.** Share one or two child-friendly bad choices you made as a child. Share how you felt after you made each bad choice. For example, you might tell kids that you were sad when you yelled at a family member. As children share bad choices that kids might make, ask them to talk about how they might feel after making a bad choice like that.

Say: **When we make bad choices, we might feel sad or like we're sinking**

Jesus loves us no matter what.

down low because we know we aren't making Jesus or our parents happy. It might make us worry that we're not loved. Let's think more about what that looks like.

Drop In the Raisins

Give each child a prepared raisin.

Encourage children, one at a time, to drop the raisins into a glass. For best results, stop at about eight raisins per glass. As children drop in the raisins, remind them of the examples they shared earlier and how they can make us feel sad like we're sinking down low. As raisins rise to the top, point them out. After the raisins lose some of the carbonation bubbles, they will start sinking again. Allow time for kids to watch the raisins as they sink and rise in the glass.

Talk About It

Ask:

- **What was surprising about the raisins?**

Say: **The raisins sank, but then they went back up! That can remind us of the son who came back to his dad. When he left home, he made bad choices that made him feel low and sad. But then he went back to his dad and he felt lifted back up. His dad was so happy to see him come back that he had a party for him. Jesus loves us like that. Even when we make bad choices, <u>Jesus loves us no matter what</u>. When we make a bad choice, we can turn back to Jesus and he'll lift us up! No matter how many times we go the wrong way, Jesus lifts us back up with his love. <u>Jesus loves us no matter what</u>.**

JESUS RAISES LAZARUS FROM THE DEAD

John 11:1-44

Supplies
- several Bibles
- "Powerful Magnets" handout (1 copy) (p. 85)
- pencil
- string
- 2 metal paper clips
- scissors
- tape
- ruler
- 2 ceramic magnets (¾ inch or larger) (available in craft stores)

Easy Prep
- Test this ahead of time to ensure your magnets are strong enough.
- Before doing anything else, review the "Powerful Magnets" handout. The photos on the handout will make this activity clear.
- Following Step 1 of the "Powerful Magnets" handout, tie 2 lengths of string to the pencil. Then tie 2 paper clips to the other ends of the string. Instead of taping the magnets to the ruler, you could use a metal ruler that the magnets are naturally attracted to.
- Following Step 2 of the handout, roll a piece of tape around your finger sticky-side out, and attach each end so that the entire outer ring is sticky. Use the tape to attach the magnet to the ruler. You'll need to attach the magnets a couple of inches apart.

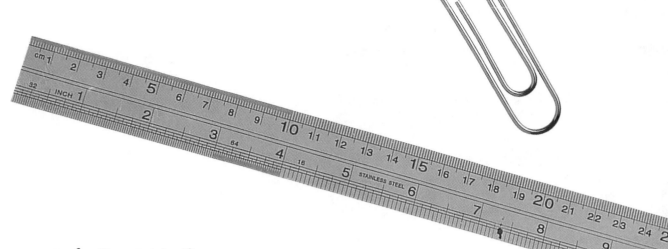

POWER OVER GRAVITY

What Kids Will Do
Kids see the power of magnets.

Watch How Paper Clips Move
Gather children together in a circle.

Say: **The Bible says Jesus did many amazing things. He even brought people back to life sometimes! One time, one of his good friends, Lazarus, had died. Jesus traveled to where he was lying there dead, and Jesus made him alive again. <u>Jesus showed that he has power over death</u>! Let's use paper clips and magnets as we think more about what Jesus' power over death looks like.**

Show children the pencil with strings and paper clips tied to it. Pass the pencil around the circle, and allow kids to each hold it and gently wave the pencil around. As they do, encourage kids to notice which way the paper clips point and what happens if they try to tilt them. Once the pencil comes back to you, say: **No matter which way you tilted the pencil, the paper clips always pointed to the ground.**

TIP!

Magnets can be dangerous for children. Avoid letting the kids play with the magnets unattended. Do not let children put the magnets near their mouths.

Make Paper Clips Float
Place two sets of evenly stacked Bibles in front of the kids. Then suspend the ruler with the attached magnets across the two stacks of Bibles, with the magnets facing down as shown in Step 3 of the handout. Remove the strings from the pencil, but keep the paper clips attached to the strings. Then hold one paper clip suspended just below the first magnet as shown in Step 4 of the handout. Tape the string to the ground or table so the paper clip floats about one-quarter inch below the magnet; then repeat with the other paper clip.

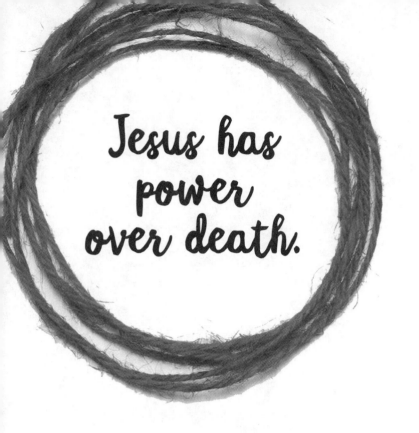

Jesus has power over death.

Allow a moment for kids to observe the paper clips floating in midair. Then remove the ruler with the magnets so the kids can watch the paper clips fall to the ground. Put the ruler with magnets back above the paper clips. Slowly lift each paper clip toward each magnet until the paper clips are suspended again.

Talk About It

Ask:

- **What surprised you in this activity?**

Say: **The magnets were really strong! They kept the paper clips up in the air. The magnets remind me of how strong Jesus is. Lazarus was lying in his tomb, dead. But Jesus lifted him up. Jesus made him alive again. That's because <u>Jesus has power over death.</u>**

POWERFUL MAGNETS

Step 1: Tie two strings to the pencil. Tie a paper clip to the end of each string.

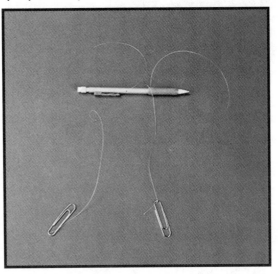

Step 2: Tape magnets to the ruler.

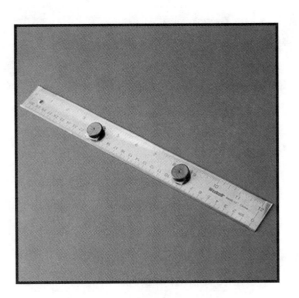

Step 3: Balance the ruler across two stacks of Bibles.

Step 4: Tape the strings so that the paper clips hover under the magnets. Slide the strings as needed.

JESUS HEALS TEN MEN OF LEPROSY

Luke 17:11-19

Supplies

- 4 identical clear glass bottles with a mouth opening at least 1 inch wide (we used Starbucks Frappuccino glass bottles)
- container of ice water
- thermos of hot water
- blue and yellow food coloring
- 2 playing cards
- paper towels

Easy Prep

- Practice this object lesson ahead of time once or twice to make sure you're proficient at placing the bottles together without them leaking too much water.
- Place 2 or 3 drops of yellow food coloring into each of 2 glass bottles. Place 2 drops of blue food coloring into each of the other 2 glass bottles.
- Immediately before the object lesson, fill the 2 bottles with yellow food coloring completely to the top with the hot water. Then fill the 2 bottles with blue food coloring completely to the top with the cold water, making sure none of the ice transfers to the clear bottles.

SEPARATION OF COLORS

What Kids Will Do

Kids see an experiment with water and colors.

Keep the Colors Separate

Gather children together.

Say: **One time Jesus met 10 men who were sick. Their skin was covered with many sores. Since other people didn't want to get sores on their skin like the men had, the 10 men had to stay away from everyone else. Let's do something to help us think about that.**

Set out one bottle filled with blue water and one bottle filled with yellow water. Explain to kids that even though the liquids are different colors, both bottles are filled with water. Place a playing card over the mouth of the bottle filled with yellow water. Hold the card in place and turn the bottle

upside down and rest it on top of the bottle with the blue water. The bottles should be positioned so that they're mouth to mouth with the card separating the liquids. Keep paper towels close by in case of spills. Carefully slip the card out from in between the two bottles while holding on to the top bottle as you remove the card.

Point out to kids that the two colors don't mix even without the card in place. Allow time for them to look at the two bottles.

Ask:
- **Tell about a time you didn't get to be with someone you love.**

Say: **The colors stayed separate from each other, kind of like how the 10 men with sores on their skin had to stay separate from other people. The Bible says that when the 10 men talked to Jesus, they even stood far away from him.** Show the children what you mean by standing across the room from them.

Jesus deserves our thanks.

The 10 men stayed away from Jesus and the others who weren't sick just like our two colors of water are doing.

Mix Up the Colors

Say: **But when Jesus made the men better, he made it so they didn't have to stay apart from their friends and families anymore. He made it so those 10 men could live with and be with other people again.**

Take the other bottles of blue and yellow water. This time, place the index card on top of the bottle with blue water before flipping it upside down to rest on the bottle with yellow water. Again, carefully remove the index card and allow time for kids to watch as the two colors of water mix.

Point to the bottles with the colors that aren't mixing. Say: **This reminds us of how the 10 men had to stay away from people because they were sick.** Point to the bottles with the colors that *are* mixing. Say: **This reminds us of**

how Jesus made the men better so they could be with all the other people. They didn't have to stay separate anymore. And that made one man so happy that he ran back to Jesus and thanked him! Jesus deserves our thanks!

Talk About It

Ask:

• **Remember the person you love who you thought of earlier? Tell what you did when you finally got to be with that person.**

Say: **Jesus didn't just make the 10 men feel better when they were sick. He made it so they could be with the people they loved. That's why one man came back to Jesus to thank him. And Jesus deserved his thanks. Jesus helped him in a big way! Jesus deserves our thanks, too. Jesus loves us and takes care of us every day!**

JESUS BLESSES THE CHILDREN

Matthew 19:13-15; Mark 10:13-16; Luke 18:15-17

Supplies
- poster board or heavy card stock
- child-safe magnets (1 for every 2 children) (see Tip below)
- paper

Easy Prep
- Cut the poster board and paper into 4x5-inch rectangles. Make 1 rectangle of poster board for each child and 1 rectangle of paper for each child.

Child-safe magnets are those that are too large for kids to swallow and aren't super magnets.

MAGNETIC ATTRACTION

What Kids Will Do
Kids use magnets to attract metal objects.

Look Around the Room
Say: **One time when Jesus was talking to a crowd of people, some children ran to Jesus, but Jesus' friends got in the way of the children. Jesus' friends stopped the kids from coming to see Jesus. But Jesus wanted to be with the children. Let's try something to help us think more about that.**

Show children a magnet. Ask children to point out things in your meeting area they think the magnet might stick to. Then test whether the magnet sticks to those things. When the children find things that the magnets are attracted to, have them put the paper and then the poster board in between the magnet and the item to see if they "get in the way" and keep the magnets from sticking. Remind the children that some people got in the way so the children couldn't come to Jesus, but Jesus wanted to be with the children.

Jesus wants to be with children.

Talk About It

Ask:

- How does it feel to know that Jesus wants to be with children?

- What do you think would be most fun about being with Jesus?

Say: **Jesus wants to be with you. He wants to stick with you like the magnet stuck to** [list items magnets stuck to in your meeting area]. **The Bible says that nothing can separate us from Jesus' love. Jesus loves you so much!**

TIP!

Magnets can be dangerous for children. Monitor children, and ensure that they don't put the magnets in or near their mouths.

JESUS HEALS BLIND MEN
Matthew 20:29-34; Mark 10:46-52; Luke 18:35-43

Supplies
- paper
- 2 metal forks
- 2 plastic forks
- glass cup or bottle
- aluminum foil
- pen that clicks
- large book

LISTENING EARS

What Kids Will Do
Kids listen to different sounds.

Listen to a Whisper
Gather children around you. Whisper as quietly as possible: **Can you hear me?** Repeat the question until most of the children are looking at you. Model cupping your hands behind your ears so children will do the same. Again whisper: **Can you hear me?**

Say: **When you put your hands behind your ears, it helps you hear a little bit better.**

Experiment With Sounds
Say: **The Bible tells us about a blind man who couldn't see Jesus but who heard Jesus was coming his way. The blind man shouted to Jesus, and Jesus heard him. Let's play with some different sounds.**

Lead children in taking turns to make various sounds with the supplies. For example, they can tap the forks together, crumple the paper and the aluminum foil, and open and close the book. Help them talk about which sounds are alike and which are different.

Jesus hears us.

Talk About It

Ask:

- Explain which was your favorite sound to make.

- What are some sounds you can make with your mouth or body?

Say: **Jesus hears all the sounds we make. He hears us when we talk to him, and he hears us when we are sad and we cry. He hears us when we sing, and he even hears what we think. No matter what—Jesus hears it all.**

JESUS MEETS ZACCHAEUS

Luke 19:1-10

Supplies

- purple cabbage (1 head)
- measuring spoons
- sealed jars or containers
- ¾ cup of vinegar or ½ cup of lemon juice
- 2 tablespoons of baking soda
- 3 large clear plastic cups
- 2 plastic spoons
- tray or cookie sheet
- sheet of white paper (optional)

Easy Prep

- At home, coarsely chop the head of purple cabbage. Then boil the cabbage in a large pot of water for 15 minutes. Drain off the liquid (but save it), and allow it to cool. Discard the cabbage. Put the purple liquid into a sealed jar or container.
- Measure out the vinegar or lemon juice and the baking soda. Place each ingredient into a small jar or container so each one is ready.
- Before kids arrive, set the 3 clear plastic cups on a cookie sheet or tray. Pour approximately ½ cup of the purple liquid into each of the cups.
- Test the quantities of each of the items ahead of time. The results will be as follows: Vinegar or lemon juice changes the purple liquid to red, and baking soda changes the purple liquid to green.

When we spend time with Jesus, he changes us.

COLORFUL CABBAGE

What Kids Will Do

Kids watch as purple water changes colors when mixed with various substances.

Watch the Liquids Change Colors

Gather children around you at a table. Place the tray with the cups on it in front of you.

Say: **I wonder if this purple water will stay purple if we add other things to it. Let's try and see what happens. Watch carefully, and tell me what you see.**

Add the vinegar (or lemon juice) to the first cup. Encourage kids to call out the color that it changed to (red). Add the baking soda to the second cup, and stir it with the spoon. Encourage kids to call out the color that it changed to (green). Leave the last container alone so kids can compare the purple water to the colors in the other cups.

Talk About It

Say: **When the purple liquid was around some things, it changed. That's like Jesus and Zacchaeus. The Bible says when Zacchaeus was around Jesus, he changed! When we spend time with**

Jesus, he changes us, too! He changes us on the inside by helping us be kind, loving, and forgiving. When we're friends with Jesus, our faces might even change because his love gives us a big smile!

Let's watch one more big change. Pour the cup with vinegar into the cup with baking soda, and let kids watch the solution grow.

TIP!

If you hold a piece of white paper behind the clear cups, kids will be able to see the color change more clearly.

Although each of these solutions interacts safely, don't combine the solutions once the object lesson is complete. Pour each solution separately down a drain, following each one with water.

JESUS' TRIUMPHANT ENTRY

Matthew 21:1-11; Mark 11:1-11; Luke 19:28-40; John 12:12-16

Supplies

- 2 white plastic disposable plates
- 5 cotton swabs
- clear liquid dish soap
- cup of water
- pepper
- paper towels
- bowl

Easy Prep

- Dip 1 of the cotton swabs in the dish soap so one end is well-coated. (Don't let the other cotton swabs touch the cotton swab with the soap.) Place all 5 cotton swabs on a plastic plate, but make sure to keep track of which one has soap on it.

POWER OF THE SCEPTER

What Kids Will Do

Kids see a special "scepter" do something amazing.

Watch Pepper React to Soap

Gather children around you at a table.

Say: **Palm Sunday is a day we celebrate how the people of Jerusalem welcomed Jesus as their king. Let's think more about what that means as we do something fun.**

Pour the cup of water onto the empty plate. Sprinkle a large amount of pepper onto the surface of the water. (Keep paper towels close by for spills.)

Say: **When I say that Jesus is the King, that means Jesus is really powerful. I have an idea. Let's see if we have anyone powerful here today. I'll test several of you to see who has power to get this pepper to move without touching it with your hands.**

Jesus is the King.

Show the cotton swabs on the plate, and hold up a dry one. Say: **Often a king has a special stick to hold. It's called a** *scepter.* **A king holds a scepter to show he's in charge and he has the power to tell people what to do. Jesus doesn't need a scepter—he doesn't need anything to make him powerful. But we're not powerful like Jesus is, so we'll need to use these tiny scepters to move the pepper.**

Choose one child to go first. Give that child a plain cotton swab off the plate. Have the child gently touch the surface of the water with the cotton swab, without stirring the water. Encourage the rest of the group to notice that nothing happens. Then have three other children also do the same thing with the plain cotton swabs, each time noticing no major changes.

Say: **I don't see anyone yet who has the power to control the pepper. I guess we should try one last time.** Choose one more child to dip the soap-covered

cotton swab into the water. Kids will notice that the pepper quickly moves away from where the cotton swab touches the water.

Say: **Wow, our friend** [name of child] **had power with that scepter.**

Pour the pepper-filled water off the plate into a bowl to dispose of later.

Talk About It

Ask:

- **What did you think when the special scepter made the pepper move?**

Say: **Only one scepter could move the pepper. It was the only powerful one. Like that, Jesus is the only real powerful King. He's not like other kings, so he doesn't need anything to help him be powerful. <u>Jesus is the King</u> of the whole world, and he's the most powerful person ever. He's powerful enough to give you everything you need. And he's powerful enough to take care of you always.**

THE POOR WIDOW'S OFFERING
Mark 12:41-44; Luke 21:1-4

Supplies
- clear plastic water bottle with lid
- water
- liquid dish soap

Easy Prep
- Fill the water bottle about ¼ of the way full. Then put the lid on tightly.

WATER BOTTLE SHAKE

What Kids Will Do
Kids see a little bit of soap turn into a lot of bubbles.

Shake the Water Bottle
Sit with children in a circle. Show children the water bottle.

Say: **Let's shake an ordinary water bottle with water in it and see if we notice anything fun or surprising.** Pass the water bottle to the child on your right. Allow time for each child to shake the water bottle and observe what happens before passing it to the next person. Encourage children to notice that although a few bubbles might form, basically the water remains unchanged and doesn't "grow."

Add Soap to the Bottle
Once the water bottle comes back to you, say: **The Bible tells us about a woman who gave just two small coins to Jesus. Even though it was only a little bit, Jesus was very happy. He knew she gave all the money that she had.**

Jesus loves givers.

Ask:

- **What do you think will happen if I put just two squeezes of soap in this bottle?**

Add two good squeezes of soap to the bottle, and put the lid on tightly. Pass the bottle to the child on your left. Encourage the child to shake the bottle as hard as possible. Have kids pass the bottle around so everyone gets a turn to shake it. Then hold up the bottle for children to see how the soap caused the water to "grow" and fill the bottle with bubbles.

Talk About It

Say: **Before we gave the water any soap, nothing happened. But when we put just two squeezes of soap in, something cool happened! That reminds me of the woman who gave just two coins. To Jesus, that was a lot! Jesus' heart was full and happy—sort of like this bottle. <u>Jesus loves givers</u>.**

THE PLOT TO KILL JESUS

Luke 22:1-6; Matthew 26:1-5, 14-16; Mark 14:1-2, 10-11

Supplies
- 2 cans of diet soda
- paper towels
- large basin or large plastic bowl

SODA SHAKE

What Kids Will Do
Kids learn what happens when a can of soda is shaken.

Gently Pass a Can
Sit with children in a circle.

Ask:

- **What are some things you could do to be kind to a friend?**

Show children the first can of soda. Say: **Let's pretend this can is one of our friends. Maybe we could even give our friend a name.** Allow time for kids to settle on a name for the can. **Let's treat [name] as kindly and gently as you would a friend.** Encourage children to pass the can of soda as gently as possible around the circle. Then open the can of soda, and allow time for children to notice what happens as you do. If kids were really gentle while passing the can, there might be a little noise but no soda will come out.

Pass Another Can
Say: **It was nice to see you be so kind and gentle. But people aren't always kind and gentle. The Bible tells about a friend Jesus had who didn't treat Jesus nicely. His name was Judas, and he**

tried to trick Jesus so Jesus would be hurt badly.

Ask:

• **What are some ways friends can hurt each other?**

Show kids the next can of soda. Have kids think of another name for this can. This time allow kids to pass the soda in whatever way they think would be fun. Children don't need to be careful or thoughtful of their "friend." Allow kids to roll it to each other or shake it up before passing it to someone else. When the can comes back to you, open the can over a large basin. Have paper towels close by for cleanup.

TIP!

Make sure to let parents know that children shook a can of soda during this object lesson so they can avoid having kids try it again at home.

Talk About It

Say: **Both of the cans looked the same on the outside. But how we treated them made a big difference. Our second "friend" was shaken up and wasn't treated gently. And when we opened it, it exploded! Being unkind to others can be a lot like that. When we say or do unkind things to others, it can make them feel really bad on the inside.**

Share a child-friendly example of a time you felt sad on the inside from something someone said or did to you. Then ask:

• **Tell about a time you felt sad on the inside because of something a friend said or did.**

Say: **Jesus wants us to be kind to our friends because he understands how we feel on the inside when someone hurts us. He knows we can feel all shaken up like our second can of soda. Jesus knows what it's like to be hurt by a friend because he's had a friend hurt him. When we're hurt or sad, we can talk to Jesus about it because we know he cares for us. Let's do that right now.** Say a quick prayer.

JESUS WASHES HIS DISCIPLES' FEET
John 13:1-17

Supplies
- dull, dirty pennies (1 per child)
- lemon juice
- bowl or plate
- paper towels (1 per child)

Easy Prep
- Pour the lemon juice into the bowl.

Jesus shows us how to serve.

SHINY PENNIES

What Kids Will Do
Kids wash dull pennies in lemon juice.

Soak Pennies in Lemon Juice
Say: **In the Bible in John 13, we can read about how Jesus washed his friends' feet. In Bible times, people wore sandals and walked on dirt roads, so their feet were often dirty and yucky. Let's wash something dirty like Jesus did.** Show kids the pennies, and point out how dirty they are.

Say: **Our pennies are dirty. Let's see if we can clean them up so they're pretty and shiny! The Bible says Jesus got out a bowl of water to wash his friends' feet. We'll use a bowl of lemon juice instead.** Have kids drop pennies into the juice.

Say: **These pennies are really dirty. I think they need to soak for a little bit before we really clean them. In a few minutes, we'll practice serving like Jesus did and we'll clean these pennies. While we wait, let's think of people who love and serve us.**

TIP!

Remind children that this lemon juice is for cleaning, not tasting, and that they should avoid putting the lemon juice or pennies in their mouths.

Ask:

- **What are some ways people serve you?** Help kids get started by sharing your own example, like having a friend help take care of a pet or a parent cook a favorite meal for your birthday.

Say: **When people serve us, they show us Jesus' love. Jesus loved his friends, and he loves us.**

Scrub the Pennies

After approximately five minutes, end your conversation and give each child a paper towel. Say: **In the Bible, Jesus got a towel and some water and washed his friends' feet so they were clean and shiny. Let's use our towels and clean the pennies.** Take a penny out of the lemon juice, and demonstrate how to place the penny on the table and wipe it with the paper towel. Encourage kids to really rub their pennies to get them clean. Spend a moment helping each

child scrub his or her penny to ensure the pennies get clean. Point out that they may even see some of the dirt from the pennies on their paper towels! Talk about how serving others can sometimes take a lot of work.

Talk About It

Ask:

- **What was it like to work to get the pennies really clean?**

- **What are other things we can clean to serve someone?**

Say: <u>**Jesus shows us how to serve.**</u> **Jesus washed his friends' dirty feet so they were clean and his friends were happy. Just like washing the pennies made them shiny, serving others can brighten their day!**

Let kids drop their pennies into your classroom offering basket or give them to the pastor as a way to serve others by giving.

JESUS IS BETRAYED AND ARRESTED

Matthew 26:47-56; Mark 14:43-52; Luke 22:47-53; John 18:1-11

Supplies
- small foam craft ball
- toothpicks (flat with smooth ends work best)
- scissors (if using round toothpicks)

Easy Prep
- If using round toothpicks, use scissors to remove the point on 1 end. Children will insert the other pointed end into the ball so only the flat end touches their hands as they toss it.

POKEY PEOPLE

What Kids Will Do
Kids create and pass a "pokey" object.

Poke In Toothpicks
Tell kids to form a big circle by extending their arms, standing so they cannot touch their neighbors, and then dropping their arms. Show kids the foam craft ball, and gently toss the ball around the circle one time. Comment on how easy it was to toss and catch the smooth ball. Say: **Good job! Passing around a smooth ball is easy, isn't it? Let's make it a little harder.**

Show children how to poke a toothpick firmly into the foam craft ball. Hold the ball and move around the circle, giving a toothpick to each child to poke into the ball. Guide the children so toothpicks are spread out around the ball, and give additional toothpicks as needed so the surface of the ball is mostly covered. Occasionally press on the toothpicks with the palm of your hand, and comment that the ball is getting pokey.

Jesus loves even his enemies.

Pass the Pokey Ball

Once everyone has added a toothpick, tell children to toss the pokey ball around the big circle again. Demonstrate how to gently toss the pokey ball to a neighbor. Have kids use only underhand throws, and caution them to throw carefully. Children may hesitate, so if someone doesn't want to catch, encourage children to skip to the next person.

Talk About It

Ask:

- **How did you feel when the pokey ball was tossed to you?**

Say: **Tossing the smooth ball was easy. We weren't nervous at all! But catching the pokey ball was a little scary because we usually want to stay away from pokey things. Sometimes people can be a little pokey or hurtful, too. People** might say or do things that hurt our feelings or make us sad.

Ask:

- **What are ways we can show Jesus' love to people who are mean?** As each child shares, let him or her remove one toothpick until all the toothpicks are gone. Briefly let kids toss the ball around again to see how showing love is better.

Say: **It's easy to love nice people, but it's harder to love people who hurt us. In the Bible, Jesus didn't run away from mean people. One time some men arrested Jesus when he hadn't done anything wrong. They hurt him badly. But he still loved them. Jesus loves everyone, even pokey people! <u>Jesus loves even his enemies</u>. His love is big enough to share with others...even pokey people!**

JESUS IS PUT ON TRIAL

Matthew 27:15-31; Mark 15:6-15; Luke 23:1-25; John 18:28-19:16

Supplies

- 2 quart- or gallon-size resealable plastic freezer bags
- new pencils with sharp tips (2 dozen or more)
- permanent marker
- large bowl
- water

Easy Prep

- Fill the resealable plastic freezer bags about ⅔ full of water.
- Use the permanent marker to draw a smiley face on one side of each bag.

SURROUNDED BY LOVE

What Kids Will Do

Kids poke pencils through plastic bags.

Things That Hurt Us

Hold up one of the water-filled bags to show the children. Say: **Look at this bag of water. It's sealed tight and the water is clear. The bag even has a smiley face! Sometimes, though, things happen that cause us to suffer or make us sad.** While still holding the top of the bag, take one of the sharp pencils and poke it all the way through both sides of the bag. Make sure some of the pencil sticks out of each side. The bag will seal around the pencil and it won't leak.

Ask:

- **What are things that hurt us and make us sad? We'll take turns saying something, and then we'll poke a pencil through the happy face.** Begin with your own child-friendly example. Then invite children to take turns sharing and poking pencils all the way through the bag. You may need to help younger kids as they poke the pencils to make sure they make it through the bag on the first try.

TIP!

This activity will work best if you hold the bag and help children guide the pencils into the bag so the pencils don't hit another pencil.

Jesus understands suffering.

Things That Hurt Jesus

When one bag is full of pencils, ask an adult or teen helper to hold it while you show the other bag.

Say: **The Bible tells about sad things that happened to Jesus. People were mean to him, and they hurt him even though he never did anything wrong. They took his clothes** (insert a pencil through the bag), **they put pokey thorns on his head** (insert another pencil), **they said mean things to him** (insert another pencil), **they hit him** (insert another pencil), **and they did other mean things** (insert a pencil).

Talk About It

Hold up both bags for the children to see.

Ask:

- **What do our two bags have in common?**

Say: **Both bags were hurt, but the water didn't leak out! Jesus suffered, and sometimes we are sad and suffer, too. When sad things happen to us, we can talk to Jesus because <u>Jesus understands suffering</u>. He knows how we feel, and his love can keep us from breaking apart. Look at the water all around the pencils! It reminds me of Jesus' love that's all around you and me.**

Ask:

- **How does Jesus surround you with love when you're sad?**

TIP!

When you've finished, place the bags with pencils still in them in a bowl in case they leak.

JESUS IS CRUCIFIED
Matthew 27:32–61; Mark 15:21–47; Luke 23:26–56;
John 19:17–42

Supplies
- paper towels (a more absorbent brand works best) (2 sections per child)
- white glue
- foam paintbrushes (1 per child)
- dark-colored washable paint
- small cups
- water
- large resealable plastic bags (1 per child)
- permanent marker

Easy Prep
- Prepare 2 paper-towel sections for each child. On 1 section, use glue to draw a heart. Wait 10-15 minutes for the glue to mostly dry, and then fold the second section over the glue drawing and pat gently. When allowing the glue heart to mostly dry before covering it with the other paper-towel section, keep in mind that if you apply the top towel too soon, it'll absorb the wet glue and reveal the heart before paint is applied.
- Put water in small cups and add about a teaspoon of paint to create a colored-water solution.

A SECRET REVEALED

What Kids Will Do
Kids paint paper towels and discover a secret picture.

Distribute Paper Towels
Give each child a prepared paper towel, a foam paintbrush, and access to the colored-water solution.

Say: **The Bible tells about the very sad time Jesus died. The Bible says the sky turned dark that day. But even though it was very sad, God had a secret plan that would make the whole world happy. Let's paint a dark sky on our paper towels. When we do, you might discover a secret that shines through the dark!**

Paint the Towel and See a Surprise
Show children how to use a foam paintbrush to cover the paper

Jesus loves us so much that he died for us.

towel in dark paint. Big strokes with plenty of water work best. As they paint, kids will begin to see the heart since the glue does not absorb the dark pigment as easily as the paper towel. Once the paper towel is covered with paint, the picture will become easier to see. Let paper towels air dry a bit. Then write each child's name on a large resealable bag and place his or her towel in the bag to take home.

Talk About It

Ask:

- **Who are people in your life who love you all the time, no matter what? How do you know they love you?**

Say: **Jesus loves us so much that he died for us. Just like the heart was always on our paper towels—even though you couldn't see it—Jesus' love was always there, even when people hurt him. And guess what! Jesus' love has always been with us, too!**

JESUS RISES FROM THE DEAD
Matthew 28:1-10; Mark 16:1-11; Luke 24:1-12; John 20:1-18

Supplies
- facial tissues (we used Kleenex brand)
- basket coffee filters (1 per child)
- washable markers
- small clear cups (9 ounce works best) (1 per child)
- cotton swabs (1 per child)
- pitcher of water
- paper plates (1 per child)

Easy Prep
- Fold a tissue in half and use a black washable marker to draw a sad face about ½ inch from the bottom of each tissue (see photos at right). Prepare 1 for each child. You can use less-absorbent paper towels instead of facial tissues or coffee filters.
- Add ¼ inch of water to each cup.
- If you leave the experiment overnight, the sad face will disappear completely as the water dries.

FROM SADNESS TO CELEBRATION!

What Kids Will Do
Kids experiment with color and water.

Place Tissues in Water
Give each child a prepared tissue.

Say: **When we cry, we use tissues to dry our tears. The Bible tells us about a time Jesus' friends were sad because he had died. But then something amazing happened! Let's see if we can make this sad face go away.**

Give one cup with a quarter inch of water in it to each child. Tell kids to place their tissues in the water with the sad face at the bottom. The water should touch the tissue but not the drawing. The water will be absorbed and slowly move up the tissue. The water will carry the color pigments with it, eventually changing the sad face into a burst of different colors. This will take about five minutes.

Ask:
- **Tell me about a time *you* were sad.** Share about a time *you* felt sad.

Note what's happening to the tissue between questions, if anything.

Ask:
- **What made you happy again?** Share your own example.

After about five minutes, ask:
- **What do you see happening to the black ink?**

Say: **When the water goes up the tissue, it separates the colors and makes the sad face go away!**

Jesus' friends were sad when he died. But he came back to life! Their sadness went away when they learned that <u>Jesus is alive now</u>! Let's use water and markers to make something bright and happy to celebrate.

Color on Coffee Filters

Give each child a coffee filter on a paper plate, a cotton swab, and washable markers. Have kids make dots with markers all over the center of the filters. Then have them dip their cotton swabs in water and touch each dot. Putting water on the bright dots will cause them to spread out and look very colorful, like fireworks!

Talk About It

Say: **The water changed our dots in surprising and beautiful ways. And since <u>Jesus is alive now</u>, he changes our lives, too. Jesus comforts us when we're sad.** Have kids give themselves a hug. **He brings happy things to our lives that give us happiness or joy.** Have kids smile and cheer. **He gives us strength when we feel tired.** Have kids make muscles. **Since <u>Jesus is alive now</u>, he makes our lives so much better!**

THE EMPTY TOMB

Luke 23:26–24:12

Supplies

- bleach
- medicine dropper (available in the pharmacy section at discount stores or at craft and hobby stores)
- small bowl
- clear jar (with a lid) filled ½ full of water
- red and green liquid food coloring

Easy Prep

- Put the lid on the jar of water.
- Fill the medicine dropper with bleach, and put it in the bowl for safekeeping.
- Because bleach removes color from fabric and other surfaces, be careful to protect your clothes and the surfaces in your classroom from coming in contact with the bleach. Practice the experiment a few times before you do it with the children.

JESUS MAKES US CLEAN

What Kids Will Do

Kids watch colored liquid change to clear liquid.

Color-Changing Experiment

Say: **Jesus is our Savior. Let's put a few drops of red food coloring in this jar to remind us that Jesus died on the cross.**

Put a few drops of red food coloring into the jar of water.

Say: **Jesus did this because he loves us and he wants us to be clean so we can meet God. Without Jesus, we're not clean because of sin, or the wrong things we do that make God sad.**

Think about something you've done that's wrong. You don't need to say it out loud. Pause. **We've all done things that make God sad. I'm going to add some drops of green food coloring to the jar to represent the wrong things we've done.** Add enough drops of

Jesus is
our Savior.

green food coloring to turn the water a dark color. You can have older children do this if you'd like.

Ask:

- **What happened to our water?**

Say: **The wrong things we do keep our lives from being clean. Without Jesus, our lives are like this water** (hold up the jar of dark water)**: yucky and not clean. But when we believe <u>Jesus is our Savior</u>, Jesus makes us clean!** Add drops of bleach until the color starts to disappear.

Say: **When Jesus' friends went to find Jesus in his tomb, he wasn't there! Because Jesus died on the cross and then came back to life, we're forgiven of all the wrong things we've done. <u>Jesus is our Savior</u> who makes us clean.**

THE ROAD TO EMMAUS
Luke 24:13-35

Supplies
- empty plastic eggs (1 per child, plus 5 for the teacher)
- dry beans
- paper clips
- jingle bells
- coins
- small Legos
- other objects small enough to fit in the plastic eggs

Easy Prep
- Prepare sample sounds by placing 5 different types of objects in 5 different eggs. Place several of each object in 1 egg so they rattle together and make a distinct sound. The leader will use these samples.
- Prepare eggs for the children so the sounds the eggs make will match the sounds the leader's egg makes. For example, if you have 15 children, make 3 eggs that each contain the same quantity of the same object the leader's egg has. Depending on your class size, more than 1 child may have an egg with the same objects inside.

SOUNDS THE SAME

What Kids Will Do
Kids try to recognize matching sounds.

Distribute Eggs
Have kids sit in a circle. Give each child a prepared egg.

Say: **Let's see how many of you are good listeners. You each have an egg, but don't open it! Instead of looking inside, we're going to *listen* to see what's inside!** Explain that you have five eggs and they all sound different when you shake them.

Shake and Listen
Say: **Ready, set, listen!** Select one of your five eggs and give it a shake. Then, one at a time, have kids each shake their eggs and decide if they sound the same as your egg. You may need to shake the sample egg again to

Jesus shows us who he is.

remind kids what they are listening for. After everyone has had a turn, have kids carefully open the eggs to reveal the objects inside and see if they heard correctly. Repeat until you have shaken and listened to all five eggs. If time allows, kids can mix up their eggs and play again.

Talk About It

Ask:

- **Why was it sometimes tricky to hear the matching sound?**

Say: **Since we couldn't see inside the eggs, we had to listen closely for the** right sound. It was tricky because we had to tune out other noises and listen carefully. The Bible tells us about two travelers who were sad when Jesus died. But Jesus came back to life! The two travelers were walking along the road when Jesus started walking with them. They didn't know it was Jesus right away. But just like we opened the eggs to see what was inside, the travelers' eyes were opened and they knew it was Jesus with them. When we read the Bible or listen to what other people tell us about him, Jesus shows us who he is, too!

JESUS APPEARS TO DISCIPLES
Mark 16:14; Luke 24:36-43; John 20:19-31

Supplies
- electric floor fan
- several uninflated balloons

Easy Prep
- Position the fan so it blows straight up into the air. Test this ahead of time, as results will vary based on fan size and speed.
- For even more fun, provide 2 electric fans and form 2 teams. Encourage teams to work together to see how many balloons they can keep in the air at once.

BALLOON FLOAT

What Kids Will Do
Kids watch balloons float in the air.

Blow Up Balloons
Say: **I've brought some balloons for us to play with today. But first I have to blow them up.** Blow up and tie the balloons in front of the kids so they can see that they aren't the special kind with helium.

Hold up an inflated balloon.

Say: **When someone drops a balloon, it usually falls to the ground.** Demonstrate. **But would you believe me if I told you that I can make these balloons float around in the air? Watch this!**

Place a Balloon Over the Fan
Turn on the fan, and set the balloon in the airstream. It should bobble in the air above the fan. Invite children to add a few more balloons and see how many can hover in the air above the fan at once. Allow time for the kids to play.

Jesus helps us believe in him.

TIP!

Balloon pieces can be a choking hazard. If a balloon should pop, quickly pick up the pieces and discard them.

Talk About It

Ask:

- **What do you think kept the balloons from falling to the ground right away?**

Say: **The fan blows air around, and the air kept the balloons up longer.** Pause. **But I didn't see the air, did you?**

We can't see air, but we know it's there because we watched the balloons bounce around in it. And we know air is there because we breathe it and it keeps us alive. Encourage kids to inhale and exhale. **We can't see Jesus with our eyes, but we still believe that he is with us all the time. The Bible tells us about one of Jesus' friends, Thomas. Thomas had trouble believing Jesus had really come back to life. He had to see Jesus to believe it. Jesus helped Thomas believe when he showed up in a locked room with Thomas and some of Jesus' other friends. And <u>Jesus helps us believe in him</u>, too!**

JESUS TALKS WITH PETER

John 13:31-38; 18:15-18, 25-27; 21:15-25

Supplies
- water (6 cups)
- liquid dish soap (1 cup)
- corn syrup (¼ cup)
- shallow tubs or containers
- plastic straws (1 per child)
- funnels (1 per child)
- cardboard tubes (1 per child)
- cookie cutters
- bubble-blowing wands in various sizes and shapes

Easy Prep
- Mix the water, liquid dish soap, and corn syrup together to create a bubble solution. Increase or decrease recipe amounts, depending on your class size.
- Pour the solution into several shallow tubs or containers that children will share.
- Feel free to experiment with other household items that blow bubbles. Our favorites, the ones that made the biggest bubbles, were straws and funnels!

THE BiGGEST BUBBLE

What Kids Will Do
Kids use different objects to blow big bubbles.

Blow Big Bubbles
Say: **The Bible tells about one of Jesus' friends named Peter. Peter followed Jesus and listened to him, but Peter also made some mistakes. He even pretended he didn't know Jesus three times! But Jesus still loved Peter and believed that Peter could do great things.**

Jesus believes in us, too. He believes in us to do great big things—even young kids! Kids may be little in comparison to big adults, but Jesus can take a little one and do great big things. Let's blow great big bubbles to help us think about that. We can try using all of these different things to help us blow the biggest bubble ever!

Jesus believes in us.

Show kids the different items available, and demonstrate how to use each one to blow bubbles. Allow kids to blow bubbles while you encourage them and comment on the bubbles' size. Point out that even though the straws are small, when you blow through them very gently, they can still make big bubbles.

Talk About It

Say: **Wow! Even small straws can make big bubbles. And even though we're small, <u>Jesus believes in us</u> and helps us do BIG things.**

Ask:

- **What big things can you do for God?** Give an example, such as helping with chores around the house or making cards to encourage others.

Say: **<u>Jesus believes in you</u> to do big things!**

TIP!

Help kids practice blowing out with straws instead of inhaling before they dip their straws into the bubble solution.

THE GREAT COMMISSION
Matthew 28:16-20; Mark 16:15-20; Luke 24:44-53; Acts 1:6-11

Supplies
- package of unsweetened drink mix
- sugar
- 2 pitchers
- drinking water
- spoon or spatula to stir drink mix
- sieve
- measuring cup
- 3-ounce cups (1 per child)

Easy Prep
- Read the directions on your drink mix to determine the amount of water and sugar you'll need, and then measure out the correct amounts without mixing them together. Set them aside.

DRINK UNMIX

What Kids Will Do
Kids mix and try to unmix a tasty drink.

Mix Drink Mix and Water
Show kids the pitcher of water.

Ask:
- **What would you say if I told you we were going to have a yummy drink today in our class?** Hold up the drink mix for the kids to see. Allow kids to respond enthusiastically.

Say: **Having a yummy drink is such a treat! Let's mix it together so we can enjoy it.**

Choose kids to help you add sugar and drink mix, and then stir to mix the drink. After the drink is mixed, stop abruptly.

Try to Separate the Drink
Say: **Oh dear. I changed my mind. Maybe we shouldn't drink all this sugar. Let's just drink water instead.**

Jesus is always with us.

Can you help me take the drink mix and sugar out?

Have a child hold the sieve over another pitcher while you pour the drink.

Talk About It

Say: **It's not working! We can't get the plain water back. It's still our yummy drink. That reminds me of a Bible story when Jesus' friends climbed a mountain—Jesus told them to meet him there. While they were all there, Jesus asked his friends to share with everyone about his love. Jesus told his friends he'd always be with them. It was kind of** like us trying to separate the water from the sugar in our yummy drink—we can't separate ourselves from Jesus.

Ask:

• **Tell some ways you think we could use to get the sugar out again.**

Say: **Once the drink is mixed, the sugar and drink mix are always with the water. You can't take them apart. Jesus is like that, too! Jesus is always with us. Let's celebrate by drinking our yummy drink now!**

Pour a drink for each child to enjoy.

Scripture Index

John

Acts

Topical Index